Holiness Demanded

Rev. Dale Burden

To order additional copies of this book, contact:

Dale Burden
5485 Larry Ave.
Virginia Beach, VA 23462
757-724-0582
Or
www.amazon.com

FWB

Dedication

To my beloved wife, Jane

Table of Contents

Forward

"The Lord's Church has confronted many conflicts in the last century. The battle of the Bible. Is it indeed the inspired Word of God? Evolution: Can it be harmonized with the Genesis account of creation? Cooperative evangelism, etc. But the damage done to the church by none of these, in my opinion, compares to that done by the church abandoning its standards of holiness.

Concern over this is what has motivated this work," so writes the author of this work. I first heard of Preacher Burden (as he is known by most) when I was a college student in the seventies. Other students spoke of him in a way that left me with the impression of Elijah the Prophet or John the Baptist. Who was this "voice crying in the wilderness?" I wondered. The subsequent years would give me an opportunity to discover for myself the man behind the reputation. The result was not disappointing. I found him to be one of the most sincere and passionate men I have ever met, especially as it concerns the purity of the church.

This book is an example of that Since the sixties there has been a Herculean attempt by the church to present Christianity in a less serious tone than it has been communicated historically. There has been a continuous effort to make authority more palatable to the taste of the common man. The result of this experiment at tweaking the church menu has not proven satisfying to any but the most ardent advocates of church marketing. The western church particularly has become increasingly worldly and ineffective at influencing the culture. One can only wonder where we would be today if the church had decided back then to realize its own ideals and establish a true Christian counter culture rather than mimic the World it is

In the face of this moral and spiritual free fall there have been voices attempting to arrest the church and turn it back to the "old paths." Unfortunately they have not been numerous enough and loud enough to hold the fort against the onslaught of the masses clamoring for change. Today the numbers of those who are deeply concerned and outspoken about the drift from the "old paths" is diminishing and their voices are being silenced. Death is claiming some and the remainder are being relegated to the sidelines of church life and treated as relics of the past who are incapable of transitioning into the new golden age of the market-driven church. In some quarters these voices have been silenced so long they are barely even tolerated. They are treated as just burrs in the saddles of the real makers and shakers in the church.

But those who trivialize these voices as legalists and relics are in danger of letting the church drift farther and farther into sin and sorrow. They are in danger of shooting their watch dog for disturbing their sleep, not knowing that a thief lurks at the door. Certainly there are some people who take fiendish delight on raining on everyone's parade. Such people are to be corrected and helped but there are others who bear a burden and a weight laid upon their hearts from God. It is not a burden that they asked for or that they delight in; it is something comparable to the prophets of old. They see more and they are compelled to speak. What they see is not a matter of how long is long and how short is short and how loud is loud. No, what they see is how holy is holiness and how humble is humility and how sinful is sin. What they see is well personified in Preacher Burden.

His love for the Savior of the World Who died for our sins has given him a keen insight into the value of a soul as well as the awfulness of sin that hardens and deceives that soul. While many preachers romance the church in order to secure their position in it, some confront the church at great cost to themselves in order to sanctify it and present it blameless to Christ. It is a lonely road these prophetic souls are called to travel.

I for one am glad Preacher Burden has chosen "the road less traveled." My hope and prayer is that he may see the fruit of his labor before his earthly journey is complete and that this book may contribute mightily to that fruitful goal. We need a revival of holiness and love.

I have felt a cleansing and a challenge as I read through these pages. I hope you will experience the same sanctifying influence as you read them. May God be glorified in His church and may this book contribute to that supreme eternal purpose.

-- Glen E. Johnson

Testimonies

It is my distinct privilege to encourage Christian readers everywhere to prayerfully contemplate the message of this book. The author of the work was my pastor for more than five years. Further, we served on church staff together for an additional fifteen plus years. Our history has convinced me that "Preacher Burden" (the name by which the writer is affectionately known) is best described by the words which Peter used to describe Noah: "a preacher of righteousness." This book is more than a sermon; it is the heartbeat of "a preacher of righteousness."

–Howard Bass, Tomball, Texas

You will be "Blessed and Benefitted" by reading HOLINESS DEMANDED.. I have known Rev. Dale Burden, a highly successful pastor and fervent personal soul-winner, for over 60 years--up close and personally. He is a devoted "Man of God", who lives what he preaches, whose ministry has blessed and helped many thousands. In this book he shares his heart and the scriptures to help Christians put into daily practice righteous, godly living that pleases our LORD. With unflinching loyalty to God and His Word, Dale writes with a heart full of love and moist eyes. I know many hundreds of preachers, but I have said for years, "I know of no one who exhibits more love for Christ and appeals to his listeners to be careful lest their deeds hurt the heart of Jesus" than Dale Burden does. The chapter on "Love for Jesus" is the key.

--Evangelist Guy F. Owens

Brother Dale Burden has been a strong voice in our movement for many decades on the subject of godly living. You may not agree with every conclusion he reaches in these pages, but we, as God's people, dare not disagree with the premise of this work. Indeed we must be admonished that "as He which hath called you is holy, so be ye holy." This is a must read for every preacher and layman. In it you will find the heart of this man of God as he presents us the challenge of "Holiness Demanded."

--Dr. Danny Baer, Academic Dean,
Southeastern Free Will Baptist College

Preface

Holiness Demanded

Follow peace with all men, and holiness, without which no man shall see the Lord. Hebrews 12:14

Have you heard the story of the parrot that lived in a bar and when a brawl broke out one Saturday night, he flew out a broken window and found refuge in the corner of a church? When the preacher came in Sunday morning, the parrot said, "Awk, new master of ceremonies." When the choir came in he said, "Awk, new floor show." When the congregation came in he said, "Awk, same old crowd." That got a laugh when I heard it many years ago. It's no laughing matter today. It is too true to be funny, especially since today we can add another sad note to it. Sad to say, increasingly the music is also similar to that of the night clubs.

The world infiltrating the church is not new. Jude warned about it long ago: *For there are certain men crept in unawares, who were before of old ordained to this condemnation, ungodly men, turning the grace of our God into lasciviousness, and denying the only Lord God, and our Lord Jesus Christ* (Jude 4). Paul sounded the same warning to the Ephesians elders (Acts 20:28-31). Tragically, what is new is the "deafening silence"—the absence of warnings against the invasion of carnality.

Vance Havner said, "Today the church is more beset by traitors within than by foes without. Satan is not fighting churches. He is joining them. He does more harm by sowing tares than by pulling up wheat. He accomplishes more by imitation than by outright opposition. The world is accepted into the church and its programs endorsed. Worldly celebrities are called in to enhance the gospel and preachers participate in the performances of the ungodly. The same popular singer combines sensuous publicity in the papers with the gospel songs in the record shops. Preachers make clowns of themselves and churches become theaters.[1]

Several years ago, Dr. A.B. Brown and I put together a booklet entitled *Recommended Reading for Christian Workers*. We printed 2000 copies for free distribution listing topics we felt would be helpful. One category was on scriptural standards of holiness for God's people. We were amazed at how little we could find in print on the subject. We had to go back to the early 1900's. Go back a few more years, however—back to the days of the Puritans and you can find plenty on this subject from writers like John Flavel, John Owen, Richard Baxter, and Charles Spurgeon's favorite writer, William Gurnall, as well as Spurgeon himself.

The Puritans

As we approach this subject of holiness, we are aware there will be resistance from today's self-centered generation regarding a plea for holy living. This is not new. God let us know long ago that *all that will live godly* [not religiously] *in Christ Jesus shall suffer persecution.* (2 Timothy 3:12) Nowhere has that been more documented than in the days of the Puritans (1550 to 1700). They lived during a period of systematic persecution. This was, not only because of their faith, but because of their very visible conscientious, godly living that always makes the worldly uncomfortable. They maintained such a testimony for Christ in an age where comforts we take for granted were totally unknown, where half the babies born died at birth and half of the adults died young. All of this seemed only to make them live with the reality of eternity more in mind and ponder the promised benefits for believers that so wonderfully exceed anything this world has to offer. With Christ as their Captain and the Cross as their banner, with kindness and humility they lived like the grace of God teaches us to live-- *denying ungodliness and worldly lusts, we should live soberly, righteously, and godly, in this present world*. (Titus 2:12)

Most in religious circles, and even many who are not, are aware that to designate someone as "puritanical" is to smear and demean them. It carries the connotation that the Puritans were religious extremists, pious to the point of being nauseating, uninformed, and an enemy of all happiness. The opposite is true. Their writings reveal they were very intelligent, humble people. They were great patriots, much involved in the welfare of their community and their country. They were men of prayer. Consider the great General Oliver Cromwell and his army who spent considerable time in prayer before every battle. Their preachers were known for tarrying long at the throne of grace before proceeding to the pulpit. They had great, orderly, disciplined families.

They sparked revivals and wielded great influence for righteousness both in England and America, and over men like John Wesley, George Whitefield, and Charles Spurgeon. Many serious students of God's Word are familiar with these names, several who will be coming up in the following pages. Many will testify to the fact, when reading after these men, they knew they were hearing from godly men who were giants in the faith. These men, and others like them, formed the foundation for the genuine revivals, not only in their days, but for the next three centuries.

In America, great revivals like those of D.L. Moody (1837 - 1899), Charles Finney (1792-1875), and Jonathan Edwards (1703-1758) of Puritan heritage and a key leader in the First Great Awakening, swelled the church rolls. Soon it became fashionable to be a church member. But as the fire fizzled, holy living suffered and church roles were increasingly composed of worldly and unregenerate members. Understandably, these demanded to be accepted. Regrettably, they were and God's command *to Cry aloud, spare not, lift up thy voice like a trumpet, and shew my people their transgression, and the house of Jacob their sins* (Isaiah 58:1) was ignored. When that is not done, sin takes over. Charles Spurgeon explained it this way:

> There has been a desperate attempt made by certain Antinomians [people who believe Christians are freed from the moral law by means of grace to get rid of the injunction which the Holy Spirit here means to enforce. They have said that this is the imputed holiness of Christ...I do not suppose that any man in his senses can apply that interpretation to the context— "Follow peace with all people, and holiness." Now the holiness meant is evidently one that can be followed like peace— and it must be transparent to any ingenuous man that it is something which is the act and duty of the person who follows it. We are to follow peace! That is practical peace, not the peace made for us, but "the fruit of righteousness which is sown in peace of them that make peace." We are to follow holiness—that must be practical holiness, the opposite of impurity, as it is written, "God has not called us unto uncleanness, but unto holiness.
>
> The holiness of Christ is not a thing to follow. I mean if we look at it imputatively—that we have at once—it is given to us the moment we believe. The righteousness of Christ is not to be followed—it is bestowed upon the soul in the instant when it lays hold of Christ Jesus! Our text speaks of another kind of holiness. It is, in fact, as everyone can see who chooses to read the connection, practical, vital holiness which is the

purport of this admonition. It is conformity to the will of God and obedience to the Lord's command. It is, in fine, the Spirit's work in the soul by which a man is made like God and becomes a partaker of the Divine Nature, being delivered from the corruption which is in the world through lust. No straining, no hacking at the text can alter it! There it stands, whether men like it or not! There are some who for special reasons best known to themselves, do not like it, just as no thieves ever like policemen or jails—yet there it stands and it means no other than what it says! "Without holiness"— practical, personal, active, vital holiness—"no one shall see the Lord."'2

The above is but a glimpse of the godly Puritans to whom we owe such a great debt. In comparison to the spiritual caliber of today's Christians, they are the giants and we are the pigmies. Any pastor willing to take the time to study their lives will agree. A good book to begin with would be Richard Baxter's *The Reformed Pastor.*

He wanted to see pastors with a love for and a good understanding of God's Word, a disciplined devotional life, and a passion for his people that would push them out among them. He embodied this among his flock at Kiddeminster where he served so effectively for years. This passion to see their people revived and changed extended to the Anglican Church, the state Church of England of which they were members until they were driven out by the Act of Uniformity of 1662. Although some say they failed in their endeavor to reform the State Church, they had a lasting influence on that denomination and left the true Church much that we desperately need to regain.

It is both strange and sad that the grace of God that *teaches us that, denying ungodliness and worldly lusts, we should live soberly, righteously, and godly, in this present world* (Titus 2:12) has been perverted into a license for sin rather than a reason to abhor and avoid it. That is exactly what has happened in this generation. Years ago, I was shocked to read of faculty members of a well-known Christian college drinking wine to celebrate the "freedom" that God's grace brought to them! Listen to sermons on radio and TV today and notice how often grace, not just salvation by grace, but grace that legalizes sin, is preached in contrast to the truth of scripture that exposes and condemns these sins.

There is no question that the majority of pulpits in America for decades have been derelict in their duty to obey Isaiah 58:1. Excuses like these are common: "If I preached like that, I'd loose my church." "Dealing with the sin causes more problems than tolerating it." The results are inevitable. When you sow to the flesh, you reap corruption (Galatians 6:7) It is true, if the clergy cried out against the sins of God's people—and named them—they would pay a price. There has always been a price to pay for standing against sin and pleading for holiness. Jesus mentioned several times about the prophets being stoned. Vance Havner said that explains why there are not many prophets, meaning those who cry out about sin. But whatever the cost, scripture is clear. God demands holiness (the word means separation) in His church.

The main attribute of God is that He is holy. Jesus, our Lord and Savior—our High Priest is *holy, harmless, undefiled, and separate from sinners.* The Father said of Him, *This is my beloved Son in whom I am well pleased.* If we are to be well pleasing to the Father, Peter tells us how: *But as he which hath called you is holy, so be ye holy in all manner of conversation, Because it is written, Be ye holy; for I am holy.(! Peter 1:15-16)*

Hebrews 12:14 does not say without perfect holiness, no man shall see the Lord. That would eliminate all of us. This holiness is a thing of growth--something we "follow." Something we desire and pursue. It is for this cause that Christ loved the church and gave Himself for her, *That he might sanctify and cleanse it with the washing of water by the word.* (Ephesians 5:26)

This is the over-arching aim of His atonement on the Cross. Regarding those "spots and wrinkles," Gurnall said, God is so determined to get rid of them that He rubs so hard "He would rather have a hole than a spot." This was the essence of Jesus' High Priestly prayer in John seventeen—*keep them from the evil...sanctify them.* Christian, pray His prayer will be realized in each of our lives. It will be if we will sincerely pray,

Lord Jesus, I long to be perfectly whole,
I want Thee forever to live in my soul,
Break down every idol, Cast out every foe,
Now wash me and I shall be whiter than snow.
-James Nicholson

Chapter One

Why We Need A New Emphasis on Holiness

Many faithful Christians are in the dark as to what is taking place in churches today. They suspect things are going in the wrong direction, but they do not realize how far it has already gone and how aggressive is the movement that is spearheading it. The following is a report from a fundamental preacher who has long been on the frontline defending the gospel. Regarding the National Pastor's Conference in San Diego, California in 2009 he wrote his observations. He was there as a reporter and noted it was sponsored by Zondervan and InterVarsity Press, two of the largest and most influential Christian publishers. Their authors represent the mainstream of evangelicalism. He listed as present men like Bill Hybels, Rick Warren, Rob Bell, and Brian McLaren. The major "Christian" magazine *Christianity Today,* was also prominently represented. The point of the article is to warn believers to beware of what these prominent leaders are advancing. The label many of them are now under is called "The Emerging Church," a very dangerous and heretical group.

Here is part of his report. It screams at us to pray for a revival that will return us to Biblical truth and scriptural holy living.

"In reality, the emerging church is simply the latest heresy within the broad tent of evangelicalism. When the 'new evangelicalism' swept onto the scene in the late 1940s with its bold repudiation of 'separatism' and its emphasis on dialogue with heretics, the door was left open for every sort of heresy to infiltrate the evangelical fold, and that is precisely what has happened.

"Coming to grips with the teaching of the Emerging Church is like trying to pin a glass marble to a table with an ice pick. It is movable and if forced to stand still and be consistent, it shatters!... there is a 'conservative' side to the emerging church issue that further complicates things. Regardless, we must deal with the emerging church because its influence is growing.

"McLaren also described Rick Warren's plunge into emerging church waters with his P.E.A.C.E. plan. When launched in April 2005, Warren said it would 'change the world.' He wants to enlist 'one billion foot soldiers' to overcome the five; 'global giants' of 'Spiritual Emptiness, Self-serving Leadership, Poverty, Disease, and ignorance (or illiteracy).' Toward this objective he is calling for a broad ecumenical and interfaith alliance of evangelicals, modernists, Roman Catholics, Orthodox, Jews, Hindus, Buddhists, homosexuals, pro-abortionists, etc. ...Rick Warren is a prominent pastor in the Southern Baptist Convention, a denomination that is permeated with emerging church philosophy.

"I attended the conference in San Diego because I am concerned about the next generation. The emerging evangelicals are targeting our children and grandchildren. Brian McLaren counseled emergents to be patient as opposed to trying to change churches overnight.

"But over time, what they reject will find or create safe space outside their borders and become a resource so that many if not most of the grandchildren of today's fundamentalists will learn and grow and move on from the misguided battles of their forebearers [Biblicist Christians]' McLaren is saying that emerging doctrine will infiltrate Biblicist churches from without through 'resources' such as books, videos, and web sites.

"This is exactly how New Evangelicalism has so deeply infiltrated fundamentalist Bible churches and independent Baptist churches over the past two decades and it is doubtless how the more radical emerging church doctrines will infiltrate them in the coming decades.

"The conference represents the fruit of the New Evangelical movement founded by Billy Graham and Harold Ockenga and the post-World War II generation of evangelical leaders who rejected biblical fundamentalism. They founded Fuller Theological Seminary and *Christianity Today*, both of which were represented at this conference.

"The emerging church aims to transform traditional biblical churches into a new emerging model and they are employing many tactics toward that end.

"One tactic is to create doubts and to bring about a re-thinking process, but they don't lead the individual back to the Bible for the answers. It is not wrong to re-think things, particularly methodology, but our thinking must be carefully bounded by Scripture or we will find ourselves in deep spiritual trouble.

"The worldliness that permeates the emerging church is breath-taking. The general sessions of the National Pastor's Conference began with half-hour stand-up comedy routines, some of it pretty crude. The comedy routines were followed by hard rock concerts complete with massive pounding speakers, colored lights, smoke, and huge rear-projection screens. All of this took place in a darkened hall. Some of the speakers, such as Will Willimon, head of the United Methodist Church, used profanities that we would not repeat in print. The females were typically dressed immodestly."[3]

In the next chapter consider why holiness must be preached and practiced by Christians.

Chapter Two

No Happiness Without Holiness

Charles Spurgeon, in his sermon on *Purging out the Leaven* from 1 Corinthians 5:6-8 put it this way: "What God has joined together, let no man put asunder. Evermore in Scripture the Doctrines of Grace are married to the precepts of Holiness. Where Faith leads the way, the virtues follow in a goodly train. The roots of Holiness and happiness are the same, and in some respects they are but two words for the same thing. There have been persons who have thought it impossible that Holiness should come out of the preaching of Salvation by Faith. If you tell men that 'There is life in a look at the Crucified One,' will they not conclude that cleanness of life is unnecessary? If you preach Salvation by Grace through Faith, and not at all by the works of the Law, will they not draw the inference that they need not be obedient to Christ, but may live as they wish?

"To this the best answer is found in the godly, honest, and sober lives of the men who are most zealous for the Gospel of the Grace of God; on the other hand, there have been others of Antinomian spirit who have dared to say that because they are saved, and Christ has finished His work for them so that nothing is left undone by way of merit, therefore, from now on they may act as they please, seeing that they are not under Law, but under Grace. Our reply is that the faith which saves is not an unproductive Faith, but is always a Faith which produces good works, and abounds in Holiness.

"Salvation in sin is not possible, it always must be Salvation from sin; as well speak of liberty while yet the irons are upon a man's wrists, or boast of healing while the disease waxes worse and worse, or glory in victory when the army is on the point of surrendering, as to dream of Salvation in Christ while the sinner continues to give full swing to his evil passions! Grace and Holiness are as inseparable as light and heat in the sun; true Faith in Jesus in every case leads to an abhorrence of every false way, and to a perseverance in the paths of Holiness even unto the end."[4]

The online Wikipedia Encyclopedia, under their section on the Puritans, has (or had, they keep changing) a paragraph on "Puritans and killjoys." Their emphasis on living holy lives was considered being a "killjoy" by the unsaved world. The Bible and history proves the opposite is true in this life and in the life to come. (1Timothy 4:8) Satan lured Eve into disobeying God. He told her God was depriving her of happiness by forbidding her to eat from the tree in the middle of Eden. He promised her she would enjoy the fruit (which she did not need) and be as wise as God if she would eat it. She ate it, gave it to her husband and he ate. That was the beginning of a trail of tears for mankind that reaches to the present. They lost communion with God and immediately found themselves in a world of thorns and wild beasts. Eve experienced severe pain in childbirth. Adam had to earn his bread by the sweat of his brow and they both wept at the death of Able, their son. They knew nothing of such misery until they sinned.

In Jesus' first recorded sermon, He linked happiness to holiness when He said, *Blessed are they that do hunger and thirst after righteousness for they shall be filled...Blessed are the pure in heart for they shall see God."* (Matthew 5:6, 8) The word "Blessed" here is plural. It means more than happiness, which depends of happenings. It refers to satisfying man's real needs and desires—*they shall be filled.* Mark it down. Without holiness there is no real happiness!

Think about why there are *pleasures for evermore* (Psalm 16:11) in heaven and misery forevermore in hell. You say, "It's because there is fire in hell and there are streets of gold in heaven." That is part of the difference, but not the main answer. The real difference is in heaven *there shall in no wise enter into it anything that defileth, neither whatsoever worketh abomination, or maketh a lie: but they which are written in the Lamb's book of life.* (Revelation 21:27) On the other hand, hell is creation's cesspool. In heaven we will have total, visible communion with our Lord. We will see Him face to face (22:4). We shall be like Him *for we shall see him as he is.* (1 John 3:2) In contrast, those who have chosen their sins instead of the Savior will hear Him say at their judgment *I never knew you; depart from me, ye that work iniquity.* (Matthew 7:23)

The truth that there is no happiness apart from holiness is often taught and illustrated in the Old Testament. Fresh out of Egyptian bondage, God promised to abundantly bless Israel if they would obey Him and severely chastise them if they did not. (Leviticus 26)   The Psalms stress the same truth. Commentators have noted the first Psalm of six verses is the text for all the following 149. The first verse of 119th Psalm does the same for that long, 176-verse Psalm. Both verses began with "Blessed" are those who live holy lives.

The vast contrast between the sinner and the saint is apparent even on this side of eternity. Paul told Timothy, *godliness is profitable unto all things, having promise of the life that now is, and of that which is to come.* (1Timothy 4:8) It's your choice. You can believe the devil who is out to devour you (1

Peter 5:8) or Jesus, who loves you and gave Himself for you. (Galatians 2:20)

There is no way a person can know true happiness when they know they are going to die and meet Jesus who loved them so much while they have grieved Him so much with their sins. No fleeting pleasure is worth that. And it is questionable how real such pleasures are. Paul wrote *she that liveth in pleasure is dead while she liveth.* (1Timothy 5:6) We read often of celebrities— those with money and fame, with opportunity to indulge in every so-called pleasure there is—finding life so miserable they commit suicide.

That believers can and do go through tough times in this life cannot be denied. Job—the oldest book in the Bible--makes that clear and also that there was a happy ending. But scripture is clear that such times do not have to rob the true Christian of his joy. Philippians has more to say about joy than any of Paul's letters, yet it was written while he was in prison. *My brethren, count it all joy when ye fall into divers temptations (James 1:2). Jesus said, Verily, verily, I say unto you, That ye shall weep and lament, but the world shall rejoice: and ye shall be sorrowful, but your sorrow shall be turned into joy. (James 1:2)*

Holiness on
Earth
is
Heaven on

Your Bible, from Genesis to Revelation, speaks of the joy of God's people when they are right with Him. When Israel turned away from their God and violated His word, they suffered. When they repented of their sins and obeyed Him they experienced revival and rejoicing. There are four minor and four major revivals in the Old Testament. The most space is given to the one during the reign of Hezekiah. The pattern there is very clear. Beginning with the clergy, there was cleansing. Widespread repentance followed. Divinely ordered ceremonies like the Passover were reinstated. There was a concerted effort to reach the lost. The result was *there was great joy in Jerusalem: for since the time of Solomon the son of David king of Israel there was not the like in Jerusalem.* (2 Chronicles 30:27)

David's case illustrates this. In Psalms 32, 38, and 51 David describes his misery during the months after his adultery. When the prophet Nathan confronted him, he repented of his sin. He tells us he prayed, *Cast me not away from thy presence; and take not thy holy spirit from me. Restore unto me the joy of thy salvation; and uphold me with thy free spirit.* (Psalm 51:11-12)

The joy and happiness that comes to believers when they live holy is linked with a number of things in scripture. Here are some of them:

- **Rejoice because your names are written in heaven –Luke 10:20**
- **Return rejoicing when you win a soul –Psalm 126:6**
- **Rejoice when you are persecuted for righteousness sake –Luke 6:23**
- **Joy when our prayers are answered –John 16:24**
- **When our spiritual children walk in truth 3 John 4**
- **Joy in giving, even out of deep poverty 2 Corinthians 8:2**
- **Joy unspeakable by believing in our Savior we have not seen –1 Peter 1:8**
- **In our Lord who is *able to keep you from falling, and to present you faultless before the presence of his glory with exceeding joy.* –Jude 24**

Again, this joy is only to those who practice holiness as defined in God's word. It is said of Jesus, *Thou hast loved* righteousness, and hated iniquity; therefore God, even thy God, hath anointed thee with the oil of gladness above thy fellows. (Hebrews 1:9, a quote from Psalm 45:7)

Isaiah, in that chapter that previewed Calvary so graphically, referred to Jesus as a *man of sorrows and acquainted with grief.* (53:3) Indeed He was, but He endured that for the *joy that was set before him* (Hebrews 12:2)—the joy of bringing many sons to glory! He spoke often of His joy. His faithful followers have the promise of one day hearing Him say, *Well done, thou good and faithful servant: thou hast been faithful over a few things, I will make thee ruler over many things: enter thou into the joy of thy lord.* (Matthew 25:21) Of that greatest of joys, on His way to the Cross Jesus said, *I will see you again and your heart shall rejoice, and your joy no man taketh from you.* (John 16:22)

Regarding the truth that there is no real happiness without holiness, the pearl of Jesus' parables—the Prodigal Son—comes to mind. After he had declared his independence from the Father and chosen to live in the "far country" we soon read *there arose a mighty famine in that land; and he **began to be in want**.* (Luke 15:14) Realizing he was going to perish if he remained there, his attitude toward the Father changed. He repented and headed home where he was royally received. Celebrating the return of one who was lost but now was found, we read *and they began to be **merry**.* (15:24) In the "far country" he began to be in **want.** In the Father's house, he began to be **merry.**

If the eyes of any unsaved person reads these pages, be reminded that the "**want**"–the lack of everything essential for life and happiness—that you now know is just beginning. If you die without Jesus as your Savior, all you will forever know in hell is endless want! Want for relief. Want for light in the outer darkness. Want for friends. Want for another chance. But in hell, no want will be satisfied. In the next chapter of Luke, Jesus lifted the lid off of that lake of fire and told us of a rich man who died and in the torments of hell made the smallest request imaginable—one drop of water to cool his tongue! He is still there and it still has not been granted.

Conversely, in that story Jesus told of a beggar who died and was carried by angels to what the Jews called heaven— Abraham's bosom. In denying the rich man's request Jesus explained *Son remember that thou in thy lifetime receivest thy good things and likewise Lazarus evil things; but now he is comforted and thou are tormented.* (Luke 16:25) For two thousand years, nothing has changed for them and never will. In eternity, the "wants" will never end for the ungodly and the righteous will forever be "merry."

Yes, Christians sometimes have tough times in this world. But nothing in this life comes close to equaling the misery of that land of outer darkness and the polluted pleasures of this world cannot compare with the *pleasures for evermore* (Psalm 16:11) we will enjoy in that land that is fairer than day. Read what Jesus said about it. Do what He said. Be ready for His return by repenting of your sins and receiving Him as you Lord and Savior.

One more truth vitally related to this topic needs to be shared here. The truly saved will be interested in this. Not only is it true that there is no happiness without holiness for Christians, but it is also true that Jesus is not happy unless those for whom He gave His life live holy.

Do you recall how God asked Satan if he had considered Job? (Job 1:8) Satan had and it irritated him that he was not able to get Job to yield to his temptations. The Lord rather rubbed it in by reminding him Job was not Satan's servant but He is *my servant* [and there is] *none like him in the earth, a perfect and an upright man, one that feareth God, and escheweth* [shuns] *evil.* It is clear

God was happy to show off His holy servant. Scripture speaks of our ability to either grieve our Savior or make Him glad. The choice is yours. You can find happiness for yourself and for Him by living holy.

Chapter Three

No Communion With Christ Without Holiness

The privilege of having communion with Christ, the Prince of the kings of the earth, the One *who washed us from our sins in his own blood and hath made us kings and priests unto God his Father* (Revelation 1:5-6) is a very high honor indeed. We should flee in horror at the hint of anything that might rob us of such a heavenly privilege. Heavenly? Yes, for complete, uninterrupted communion with Him is what makes heaven, heaven.

God's desire and plan has always been to have communion with us. He loves us and made us in His likeness and image so He could communicate with us. That is not true of any other creature. In the opening chapter of the Bible we read of God talking with Adam and Eve there in the fabulous Garden of Eden (Genesis 1:27, 28). How precious must have been the communion of that holy couple with their holy Creator! Even after sin had severed that blessed relationship, that holy God graciously sought them out and provided a way for that blessed relationship to be restored. If that communion was again to be real, these opening chapters made it clear that sin had to be addressed.

That theme permeates all scripture. Fast forward to Israel's exodus from Egypt (Exodus 14). Soon they were at Mount Sinai where they would learn, above everything else, God is an awesome and holy God. Mount Sinai was altogether on smoke. (Exodus 19:18) "That vast isolated mountain-block-- two miles in length and one in breadth seemed all on fire! As 'the smoke of a furnace' it rose to heaven, 'and the whole mount quaked greatly and 'there were thunders and lightning and the voice of the trumpet exceeding loud. But, more awful than any physical signs, Jehovah came down upon Mount Sinai and Jehovah called Moses to the top of the mount, and God Himself 'spake all these words' of the commandments. For three days had the people been preparing by continued sanctification, and now they stood in readiness at the foot of, although shut off from, the mountain. But even so, 'when the people saw it, they removed, and stood afar off.'"[5]

There God gave His people His holy Law, directing them in how they were to worship Him and also the pattern for the Tabernacle, the place where they were to worship. Exodus ends with the erection of that precisely and divinely designed tent. The great tent—the most elaborate and expensive edifice of its kind ever erected, was "the tent of meeting" where God met with His redeemed people. It contained two rooms, the Holy Place and the other, separated by a heavy veil, the Holy of Holies. Once a year, on the Day of Atonement, the High Priest alone entered that room. It was constantly filled with brilliant, supernatural light that shined on the images of angels woven in gold into the beautiful curtains.

Like no other spot on earth, it symbolized God's Holy presence. Strict guidelines were given on how the High Priest alone was to enter. God meant what He said. One day, two sons of Aaron's, the High Priest, decided to go in their own way. Instantly, fatal fire from God struck them. The story is found in Leviticus 10. It made lasting impressions on God's people. Tradition says, after that even when the High Priest entered, he had a rope tied around him so, if he were slain, they could pull him out without having to try to go in. The Lesson: We come to the Holy God on His terms or we cannot come at all!

We are speaking of communion with a Holy God. We believe we are communing with God when we pray. That is not so if we come while living in disobedience. *He that turneth away his ear from hearing the law, even his prayer shall be abomination.* (Proverbs 28:9) You will be like the Pharisee in Luke 18:11, who *stood and prayed thus with himself, God, I thank thee, that I am not as other men,* Chapters 21and 22. To a generation of His people who had been enslaved all their lives and almost none of them could read or write, God thus taught them that holiness is essential for His people to commune with Him.

So what is communion with Christ? Scripture sometimes speaks of two "walking together." Amos asked, *Can two walk together, except they be agreed?* (3:3) The answer is apparent. Both must be agreed on the direction they are taking. One must be the leader. For the Christian, that must be Jesus. We must trust Him. He knows the path we are to take. In John Bunyan's *Pilgrim's Progress*, Christian found himself in grave danger when he took By-Path Meadow and arrived fearful and despondent in the devil's dungeon.

For two to walk together in communion requires that they both like each other. That is true in our homes. Christian couples who are angry and at outs with each other are certainly not going to enjoy what God intended for us when He made matrimony His plan. The same is true if we do not truly love Jesus.

The beloved apostle John had enjoyed the communion with His Lord for many years when he wrote the letter of First John. Desiring this for his fellow believers that your joy may be full (1:4), he wrote *If we walk in the light as he is in the light, we have fellowship one with another, and the blood of Jesus Christ, his son cleanseth us from all sin.* (1:7) He continued by saying *If we say we [including himself] have no sin we deceive ourselves and the truth is not in us.* (1:8) and added *If we confess our sins, he is faithful and just to forgive us our sins and to cleanse us from all unrighteousness.* (1:9) In the next chapter he said, *I write unto, that ye sin not. And if any man sin, we have an advocated with the Father, Jesus Christ, the righteous.* (2:1)

These verses underscore the truth that holiness of life is essential if we are to enjoy fellowship and communion, not only with Christ, but with fellow believers. This purity of life is not merely the original purging of our sins at the time of salvation. As evident in the continued action of the word "cleanseth" in verse 7, we are in need of constant cleansing. That is constantly available on the merits of the blood of Jesus Christ when He died for our sins on the Cross.

Many think of having their sins washed away when they were saved, but then they walk in a dirty world and have to go back, maybe during a revival, and get washed again. Instead, think of it this way. When you were saved, you didn't just get cleansed. You received the **Cleanser**. He lives in you. As we continue to trust Him, He continues to cleanse you. It is somewhat like your eyes. Skin on your face is oily. It collects dust during the day. But two spots on your face stay clean—your eyes. They are washed all day long. That does not eliminate the need to confess the sins of which the Holy Spirit convicts us (Verse 9). It is clear, fellowship and communion with Christ and the family of God are possible, but they require constant cleansing and confession.

This need for constant cleansing is seen in what Jesus instituted at the Last Supper. Our Great Teacher, by His actions and His instructions, taught us that night what it means to truly have communion with Him. At the traditional Passover meal, Jesus broke unleavened bread, gave it to His apostles, and instructed them to eat it. He said that bread, made from grain that had its life crushed out of it, represented His body soon to be broken and made lifeless. He then passed them a cup containing juice—the fruit of the vine (never called wine in this ordinance)—a suitable symbol of His blood that was soon to be shed to atone for our sins.

In that same service, Jesus added something entirely new--the washing of the saints' feet. Yes, it was an act of humility, and His servants were going to need that as they took His gospel to the world. But the primary lesson was to teach us our need for daily cleansing.

Three times in this passage Jesus used the word "clean." The lessons from that initial Communion service are these: (1) Communion with Jesus is possible because of the merit of His shed blood and broken body that atoned for our sins and became efficacious for us when we received Christ as our Savior. (2) Communion with Christ also requires continual cleansing. The cleansing at the time of salvation is like a bath. Walking in a dirty world our feet would need to be washed often. This regular, daily cleansing is pictured in the ordinance of feet washing. This is why Paul said before believers take Communion, we need to first examine ourselves to see if there is sin in our lives (1 Corinthians 11:28). Together, these two parts of the same service illustrated how we have communion with Christ. Salvation is pictured in what is provided in the cup and the broken bread while daily cleansing is portrayed in the washing of their feet.

We do not wish to discourage fellow believers by stressing the fact holiness is essential. Anyone who has truly been born again should not be discouraged by the fact God has instructed us to follow holiness and said we cannot see God without it. Instead, we can be encouraged for He has made cleansing available. Listen to the inspired words of Peter: *According as his divine power hath given unto us all things that pertain unto life and godliness, through the knowledge of him that hath called us to glory and virtue: Whereby are given unto us exceeding great and precious promises: that by these ye might be partakers of the divine nature, having escaped the corruption that is in the world through lust.* (2 Peter 1:3-4)

Please note the following highlighted phrases. God's promises are available to us. They are sufficient for everything that pertains to *life* and godliness. At conversion, we were made *partakers of His divine nature.* That new nature yearns to be like Jesus. All of this enables us to escape the corruption in this world. Other passages like Romans chapters 6 and 8 sound this same truth. We can have victory over sin! No, that is not sinless perfection. But we dare not read that and continue to justify our carnal conduct claiming we can't help it. Enoch walked with God (Genesis 5:22). That was more than a little jaunt. He walked with God continually for centuries. He did and we can and we must. There can be no real happiness or communion with Christ without holiness. Loss of that is too high a price to pay. Study the Scriptures to see what it cost those who would not live holy whose stories are told there.

David had seen what happened to King Saul when the Spirit of God left him. He didn't want that! After his sin with Bathsheba, in his prayer of repentance, pleading for forgiveness, he especially prayed *Cast me not away from thy presence; and take not thy holy spirit from me.* (Psalm 51:11) David--the man *after his* [God's] *own heart*--knew God's presence (Psalm 23:4 *thou art with me*). He never wanted to loose communion with his Lord. If you value His presence, *Ye that love the Lord, hate evil.* (Psalm 97:10).

Chapter Four

No Answered Prayer Without Holiness

David knew a lot about prayer. He wrote *I love the Lord, because he hath heard my voice and my supplications. Lord in distress: the Lord answered me, and set me in a large place.* (Psalm 116:1-2 118:5) He knew something else also. He learned *If I regard iniquity in my heart, the Lord will not hear me*. (Psalm 66:18)

The Bible states this truth repeatedly. Isaiah reminded the obstinate people of his day *Behold, the Lord's hand is not shortened, that it cannot save; neither his ear heavy, that it cannot hear, But your iniquities have separated between you and your God, and your sins have hid his face from you, that he will not hear.* (59:1-2)

Preparing His apostles for the coming crisis of seeing Him crucified and then ascend back to heaven, in John 15:7 and 10, Jesus assured them He would answer their prayers. He said *ask what ye will and it shall be done unto you.* However, He set conditions. They had to abide in Him and His words abide in them and they must keep His commandments. Years later, John echoed these words when he wrote *And whatsoever we ask, we receive of him, because we keep his commandments, and do those things that are pleasing in his sight*. (1 John 3:22)

True believers who have followed the Lord and been involved in serving Him know our God hears and answers prayer. There is no argument about this truth. We have proven His promises too many times. But we know also there are times when we have prayed earnestly and our prayers have gone unanswered. At such times David's prayer is appropriate: *Search me, O God, and know my heart: try me, and know my thoughts: And see if there be any wicked way in me.* (Psalm 139:23-24)

God is neither unkind nor unwise when He does not answer our prayers. Parents are right in not giving a disobedient child everything he asks. God is a good and wise Father when He does the same. James tells us that our prayers go unanswered when our motives are wrong: *Ye ask, and receive not, because ye ask amiss, that ye may consume it upon your lusts.* (4:3) Our prayers themselves may be stained. A person may pray a prayer for revenge against another. Such action, while on our knees is a heinous sin. God is right in not answering such requests.

**Unless you live holy,
you will be wholly
without answered prayer!**

Did you know Jesus prayed a prayer that was not answered? *O my God, I cry in the day time, but thou hearest not; and in the night season, and am not silent.* (Psalm 22:2) This Psalm pictures Christ on the Cross. It was written almost a thousand years earlier. It presents such an accurate picture of Jesus' suffering in order to make atonement for our sins that some commentators have labeled it "the fifth gospel." But how is it Jesus, God's Son, could pray a prayer that His Father would not answer? Because on the Cross He took the sinners' place. There He bore our sins: *Who his own self bare our sins in his own body on the tree.* (1 Peter 2:24) With all our iniquity laid on Him (Isaiah 53:6), Charles Spurgeon wrote, 'He was not heard, because we as sinners did not deserve to be heard; He was not heard that we might be heard."

Have you ever wondered what you would do if you couldn't pray? Or if you tried to pray and knew it wasn't going to do any good? You don't ever want to be in that position!

Remember Saul's case: *Samuel said to Saul, Why hast thou disquieted me, to bring me up? And Saul answered, I am sore distressed; for the Philistines make war against me, and God is departed from me, and answereth me no more.*
(1 Samuel 28:15)

Christian, we must be faithful in prayer before the throne of grace. Someone has said, "Every failure is a prayer failure." In His Word, our caring heavenly Father has told us not to worry *but in everything by prayer and supplication with thanksgiving let your request be made known unto God.* (Philippians 4:6). In Luke 18, Jesus taught us *always to pray and not faint* [quit]. In Luke 11, observing Jesus praying, His disciples asked Him to teach them to pray as John the Baptist taught his followers. In response, Jesus gave us "The Lord's Prayer," or more accurately, "The Model Prayer." Jesus taught us to pray for our enemies and those who despitefully use us and in His first prayer on the cross He did just that. He asked us to pray for one another and for laborers for the harvest field. The list is as endless as our needs and the answers as boundless as His love.

Remember how Jesus prayed. In Gethsemane He prayed in such agony, He sweat great clots of blood. He prayed for us when He was on earth (John 17:20). He is still praying for us *seeing he ever liveth to make intercession for them* (who come to Him by faith. (Hebrews 7:25).

Whatever keeps us from being men and women of prayer is surely the most destructive thing we face. O those wretched robbers that keep us from accepting the invitation of our High Priest *who is touched with the feelings of our infirmities and is tempted in all points as we are*, who graciously opens the door to His throne room to the only place, yes, and to the only Person where we can *obtain mercy, and find grace to help in time of need.* (See Hebrews 4:16-17).

Christian, you cannot survive in this world without praying prayers that get answered! Prayer is our breath! Unless you live holy, you will be wholly without answered prayer! We must not forget, it is *The effectual fervent prayer of a <u>righteous</u> man availeth much.* (James 5:16).

Chapter Five

No Effective Soul Winners Without Holiness

The fruit of the righteous is a tree of life; and he that winneth souls is wise. (Proverbs 11:30)

"The two things are put together—the life first, the effort next: what God has joined together let no man put asunder." -Charles Spurgeon

As believers we are left in this world to win souls to Christ for the glory of God. *Herein is my Father glorified, that ye bear much fruit; so shall ye be my disciples. (*John 15:8) This was Jesus' last command—His Great Commission to us. (Mathew 28:18-20) To equip us for this great task Jesus promised *ye shall receive power, after that the Holy Ghost is come upon you: and ye shall be witnesses unto me both in Jerusalem, and in all Judaea, and in Samaria, and unto the uttermost part of the earth.* (Acts 1:8)

The Holy Spirit is the One who converts us. This happens when we repent of our sins and place our faith in Jesus' finished work on the Cross. That's when we are born again of the Spirit. (John 3:3-6) He begins that work by convicting people of their sins. *When He is come, He will convict the world of sin, and of righteousness, and of judgment.* (John 16:8) There is no human way we can convict or convert people. We can plant the gospel seed. We can water it with our prayers and our tears. But it is God alone who gives the increase. (1 Corinthians 3:7) We must grasp this truth and abide by it. We must have the power of the Holy Spirit or we will be sowing to the flesh. That is why Jesus instructed His disciples *to tarry ye in the city of Jerusalem, until ye be endued with power from on high.* (Luke 24:49)

Even Jesus, when John the Baptist baptized Him and He began His public ministry, had the Holy Spirit come upon Him. (Matthew 3:16) Luke tells us how Jesus carried out His entire ministry in the power of the Holy Spirit: *God anointed Jesus of Nazareth with the Holy Ghost and with power: who went about doing good, and healing all that were oppressed of the devil; for God was with him.* (Acts 10:38)

When we read the book of Acts we are amazed at the huge numbers of converts! Three thousand on that first day the believers were all filled with the Holy Spirit! Pentecost—though, like Calvary, will not be repeated, but it is the <u>pattern </u>for the New Testament church. This writer has read the book of Acts--that book on *methods* for the Church-- scores of times, asking the question, "How did they do it?" They reached the then-known world in one generation! The inescapable answer is found in the first two chapters: persistent, persevering <u>prayer</u> and the <u>power of the Holy Spirit.</u> That permeates the entire book of Acts.

The previous section dealt with prayer and how holiness is essential if we are to get our prayers answered. So how about the matter of having the Holy Spirit's power in our lives in order to effectively win souls to Christ? Acts 5:32 gives the answer: *we are his witnesses of these things; and so is also the Holy Ghost, whom God hath given to them <u>that obey him.</u>*

So God gives the Holy Spirit only to those who obey Him! That means those who live holy. What else would you expect? Remember, He is the <u>HOLY </u>Spirit. He is not going to anoint unholy vessels. Listen to God pleading through Isaiah, the Prince of the Old Testament prophets: *Depart ye, depart ye, go ye out from thence, touch no unclean thing; go ye out of the midst of her; <u>be ye clean, that bear the vessels of the Lord</u>.* (52:11)

Consider the phenomenal ministry of John the Baptist. We are told Jerusalem, all Judea, and the whole region of the Jordan went out to the riverbank to hear him preach. (Matthew 3:5) King Herod wanted to kill him, but was afraid to do so because the multitude counted him a prophet (14:5). Jesus said of John that he was more than a prophet and *Of them born of woman, there hath not risen a greater than John the Baptist.* (11:9-11).

Now listen to the explanation of that awesome influence John had on the wicked King Herod: *Herod feared John, knowing that he was a just man and an holy, and observed him; and when he heard him, he did many things, and heard him gladly.* (Mark 6:20) That is amazing, especially when we are told *And many resorted unto him, and said, John did no miracle: but all things that John spake of this man* [Jesus] *were true.* (John 10:41)

Unholy people can talk about winning souls, but in the end they will discover all they have is wood, hay, and stubble! Unfruitful, they learn they are therefore unwise. Read the biographies of great soul winners. Such men are *wise*--not fools.

Remember Proverbs 11:30

The fruit of the righteous is a tree of life; and he that winneth souls is wise.

Beloved, we must be wise. We must win souls. Some spend their time making sand castles or forming statues of ice. The tide will destroy the sand castles and time will melt the ice statues *But he which converteth the sinner from the error of his way shall save a soul from death and shall hide a multitude of sins.* (James 5:20) That is indeed a wise man and God has promised that *they that be wise shall shine as the brightness of the firmament; and they that turn many to righteousness as the stars forever and ever.* (Daniel 12:3)

What an honor and a joy it is to win a soul! It is an honor and joy unholy lives do not deserve nor will they ever enjoy. Conversely, holy hearts can for they have God's word on it: *They that sow in tears shall reap in joy. He that goeth forth and weepeth, bearing precious seed, shall doubtless come again with rejoicing, bringing his sheaves with him.* (Psalm 126:5-6)

There are many ways to reach out to lost souls. Hear again the prince of preachers:

> "Let me commend to you, dear friends, the art of button-holing acquaintances and relatives. If you cannot preach to a 100, preach to one! Get a hold of the man, alone, and in love, quietly and prayerfully, talk to him. 'One! you say' Your Master was not ashamed to sit on the well and preach to one and when He had finished His sermon, He had really done good to all the city of Samaria, for that one woman became a missionary to her friends!... it must not be tolerated that Christ should be unknown through our silence, and sinners unwarned through our negligence!... This is one of the most honorable modes of soul winning.
>
> "Beloved, we must win souls! We cannot live and see men damned! We must have them brought to Jesus! Oh, then, be up and doing, and let none around you die unwarned, unwept, unprayed for! A tract is a useful thing, but a living word is better; your eyes and face, and voice will all help; do not be so cowardly as to give a piece of paper where your own speech would be so much better. I charge you to attend to this for

Jesus' sake. Some of you could write letters for your Lord and Master. To far-off friends a few loving lines maybe most influential for good."[6]

The only thing that can make heaven sweeter is to win souls and have them with us. Paul understood that when he said *I am made all things to all men that I might by all means save some.* (1 Corinthians 9:22) He said of those he had won in Thessalonica , *what is our hope, or joy, or crown of rejoicing? Are not even ye in the presence of our Lord Jesus Christ at his coming?* (1 Thessalonians 2:19) Believer, be wise. Win souls. That means you must live holy.

UNLESS WE SEE SIN AS SERIOUS WE WILL NEVER BE MOVED TO BE A SOUL WINNER.

We are all too prone to take our Lord's great and final commission to us too lightly. After His resurrection, He directed all His followers *to Go ye into all the world, and preach the gospel to every creature.* (Mark 16:15) It is just as necessary that the unsaved hear the gospel as it was for Jesus to die to provide the gospel. If you are saved, someone brought you that saving story.

The early Christians took that seriously and, after obediently waiting in earnest prayer for ten days, all hundred and twenty in that upper room were filled with the Holy Spirit's power as Jesus had promised (Acts 1:8). They immediately filed into the streets in Jerusalem and told the crowds who were there to celebrate the Feast of Pentecost of salvation through the atoning death of Jesus on the Cross fifty days previously. Thus the church was born and three thousand souls were added to the church that day.

Their zeal to tell others the good news did not end that day. In spite of opposition and even deadly persecution, while some carried the body of their beloved deacon Stephen to his burial, the others went everywhere preaching the gospel. (Acts 8:1-2)

Through the centuries, the church has lost its zeal to go after the lost sheep and have suffered greatly for that dereliction of duty. Yet, God in His mercy, from time to time, has raised up men like William Carey, David Livingston, and Hudson Taylor to earnestly and tearfully remind the redeemed of our responsibility to obey our Lord's commission. We need to read and heed those earnest pleas and ask God to again raise up such voices in our midst. Two truths will stand out in their pleading: (1) The fact we will one day stand before Jesus, our Judge, and answer for how we have responded to His command. (2) We must have the power of the Holy Spirit in order to effectively carry out His command and He will give that essential power only to those who obey Him. (Act 5:32) That's how holy men and women become effective in the harvest. O God, forgive us and deliver us from our barrenness!

Christian, let this story and this song challenge you to begin today to get where you need to be in order to be a soul winner.

Charles C. Luther (1877) heard Rev. A. G. Upham tell the story of a young man who was about to die. He'd only been a Christian for a month, and was sad because he'd had so little time to serve the Lord. He said, "I am not afraid to die; Jesus saves me now. But must I go empty hand-ed?" This incident prompted the writing of the word of the song below. Stebbins wrote the music when Luther gave him the words. The complete song was first published in *Gospel Hymns No.3*, 1878.

> Must I go an empty-handed?
> Must I meet my Savior so?
> Not one soul with which to greet Him?
> Must I meet my Savior so?
> --Charles C. Luther

Needed Instructions for the Soul Winner

Until now, the emphasis has been on how holiness is essential in the life of the believer if he or she is to be a successful soul winner. Unless our lives are characterized by holy living, few are even going to try to talk to others about their need of Christ. But along with a holy life we need our heads filled with Bible truth. We don't have to have a college degree in theology, but we must be clear on who Jesus is, what He did for us to make salvation possible, and what we must do to be saved. After a brief summary on who Jesus is and why He can forgive us when we receive Him as our Lord and Savior, the matter of repentance will be addressed. There is much confusion and outright error regarding repentance today.

Who Is Jesus Christ? To be saved, a person must know the correct answer to that question. Jesus asked the religious leaders of His day, *What think ye of Christ? whose son is he?* (Matthew 22:42) He knew it was essential that the apostles were clear on this and asked them *Whom do men say that I the Son of man am?* And then, *But whom say ye that I am?* (Matthew 16:13, 15)

The clear, non-debatable, non-negotiable, answer from God's Word is He is the Son of God, the Second member of the holy Trinity, with all the attributes of deity, who chose to come into this world in human flesh through the womb of a virgin. That happened on that first Christmas approximately 2000 years ago. He spent the next thirty-three and a half years living without sin, and during the final few years, by miracles that cannot be duplicated or disproven, making it clear He is indeed God manifest in the flesh.

He revealed the Father to us, taught us how we can be saved, how to live, and after dying on the cross for our sins, and coming out of the tomb alive three days later, He stayed on earth forty more days to give us many *infallible proofs* (Acts 1:3) that He is alive forever more. Then, before returning to the Father in heaven, He gave us our marching orders to go into all the world, make disciples and baptize them in the name of the Father, Son, and Holy Ghost (Matthew 28:19, 20). Having provided full payment for the sins of the world (1 John 2:1) *when he had by himself purged our sins, sat down on the right hand of the Majesty on high* (Hebrews 1:3) where He is today as our constant Advocate (1 John 2:1) and Intercessor. (Hebrews 7:25)

He is *the way, the truth, and the life*—the One and only Savior for sinners. Therefore He could truthfully say *no man cometh to the Father but by me.* (John 14:6) When He came to this world to atone for our sins, most people rejected Him, *But as many as received him, to them gave he power to become the sons of God, even to them that believe on his name.* (John 1:12) The words "receive" and "believe" are used interchangeably with regard to salvation. When we by faith receive the Christ of the Bible as our Savior, it is because we believe Him. That brings us to the other vital matter we must clearly understand if we are indeed going to be soul winners.

Repentance and Salvation: Both Jesus (Matthew 4:17) and John the Baptist (Matthew 3:2) began their ministries preaching repentance. Twice in Luke 13 Jesus said *I tell ye Nay: but except ye repent ye shall all likewise perish.* (Verses 3 and 5) While scripture is clear that salvation is by grace alone through faith alone in Christ alone and in almost 150 verses it is stated by faith (by believing), careful study will reveal repentance is included in the act of believing or placing our faith in Christ. This is clear from Paul's statement in 1 Thessalonians 1:9: *Ye turned to God from idols.* Repentance and faith cannot be separated. To turn to God is to turn from idols (sin). It is two decisions in one like it was at Jesus' trial when Pilate offered to free Jesus or Barabbas. When they chose Barabbas they automatically rejected Jesus. See it in these verses: *Repentance toward God, and faith toward our Lord Jesus Christ.* (Acts 20:21) *Ye repented NOT ... that ye might* *believe Him.* (Matthew 21:32)   Many more such passages could be cited.

For a good definition of repentance see Ezekiel 18:30: *Repent, and turn yourselves from all your transgressions; so iniquity shall not be your ruin.* But let me be clear. Repentance is not a turning from sin in the sense of changing you own life. You cannot do that. Only the Holy Spirit can do that through the New Birth. Repentance is godly sorrow over our sins (2 Corinthians 7:10) produced by the Holy Spirit's conviction to the point we are willing to surrender our lives to Him thereby turning from our sins as in 1 Thessalonians 1:9: *For they themselves shew of us what manner of entering in we had unto you, and how ye turned to God from idols to serve the living and true God.*

Hopefully, everyone reading these pages understands that every person who has ever been saved or will be saved is saved by the atoning death of Jesus on the Cross to pay for our sins. This is just as true of the Old Testament saints as it is in the New Testament. In the Old Testament, they were saved by faith looking forward to and believing God would supply a Savior as He had promised. In the New Testament age, we are saved by looking back on the fulfillment of those promises as they became realities in Jesus' death on the Cross at Calvary. Also, in both the OT and the NT, repentance of sin was essential. That is clearly seen in Isaiah 55:6-7: *Seek ye the Lord while he may be found, call ye upon him while he is near: Let the wicked forsake his way, and the unrighteous man his thoughts: and let him return unto the LORD, and he will have mercy upon him; and to our God, for he will abundantly pardon and he will have mercy upon him; and to our God, for he will abundantly pardon.*

The invitation to receive free salvation is extended to everyone. (See Isaiah 59:1) Repentance is clearly seen as a requirement. The "wicked" is instructed to "forsake his way" and "the unrighteous man his thoughts" and return to God. Faith is also evident here for only if these seekers believed God's promises would they seek Him. That salvation is entirely by God's grace and not man's works is seen in the fact God has mercy on the repenting sinner and grants him abundant pardon. The passage wisely and earnestly urges the unsaved person to *Seek ye the Lord while he may be found, call ye upon him while he is near* (Verse 6), pointing to the reality that the time will come when He will not be near and cannot be found. Anyone reading these lines, who is not certain, according to the Scriptures, that they have Christ as their Savior, should heed that verse now.

Repentance Involved in the Sin of Mistreating Jesus

In his sermon from Jesus' statement in John 15:25, *They hated me without a cause*, Spurgeon made this so clear. He said, "I come to dwell on MAN'S SIN, that he should have hated the Savior without a cause. Ah, Beloved, I will not tell you of man's adulteries and fornications and murders and poisonings and sodomies. I will not tell you of man's wars and bloodsheds and cruelties and rebellions. If I want to tell you of man's sin, I must tell you that man is a deicide—that he put to death his God and slew his Savior!

"And when I have told you that, I have given you the essence of all sin—the masterpiece of crime—the very pinnacle and climax of the terrific pyramid of mortal guilt. Man outdid himself when he put his Savior to death...when it slew the Lord of the Universe, the Lover of the race of man who came on earth to die! Never does sin appear so exceedingly sinful as when we see it pointed at the Person of Christ whom it hated without a cause!"[7]

Jesus died for all of our sins and all of us were guilty of this most heinous of all sins. When the Holy Spirit brings conviction to a sinner's heart and helps him see how he has mistreated—indeed hated Jesus without a cause--that brings repentance like nothing else. Finding forgiveness from that sin of all sins is what makes a Christian love the Savior and want to please Him. Failing to help sinners see this and repent of it is why so many make decisions that do not stick. Sorry for the sin of mistreating others or abusing yourself with drugs, liquor, etc., pales in comparison to seeing what we have done to Him.

Jesus said *to whom little is forgiven, the same loveth little.* (Luke 7:47) That person who has come to grips with the colossal sin of how he has mistreated Jesus, who has faced it, confessed and forsaken it, will love Jesus deeply. In contrast to most who go to the altars today, that person will very likely be back next week, next year, and for years to come. In our soul winning, we need to emphasize that repentance involves this sin of all sins. It is not merely the person has been out of church, succumbed to the usual social sins, abused their body and broken some of the Ten Commandments. He needs to see that his sin has broken Jesus' heart and made it necessary for Him to go to the Cross to atone for those sins. Listen to what the great evangelist D. L. Moody said about the lack of real repentance:

> "When a man is not deeply convicted of sin, it is a pretty sure sign that he has not truly repented. Experience has taught me that men who have very slight conviction of sin, sooner or later lapse back into their old life. For the last few years I have been a good deal more anxious for a deep and true work in professing converts than I have for great numbers. If a man professes to be converted without realizing the heinousness of his sins, he is likely to be one of those stony ground hearers who don't amount to anything. ... I believe we are making a woeful mistake in taking so many people into the Church who have never been truly convicted of sin. Sin is just as black in a man's heart today as it ever was."

-- (D.L. Moody, "Results of True Repentance,"
from *The Overcoming Life and Other Sermons,*
1896).[8]

**We need to stress the importance of repentance in light
of the following popular errors being taught today:**

**(1) That the unsaved are dead in their sins and dead
people can't repent.**

When Adam and Eve sinned, they became fallen and sinful
but they were still human beings. They did not become rocks or
robots. Although they lost their right standing with God,   they
still had volition and were able to think and repent. Such is
essential to being human.   Some have gone so far as to say until
a person is saved he is nothing more than an animal. Scripture
explains the change that takes place when we are born again by
saying we become new creatures in Christ Jesus. We *put on the
new man, which after God is created in righteousness and true
holiness.* (Ephesians 4:24)   That is the big change, not that a
"rock" or "animal" has now become a saved human being.

When I was in Graduate School, I had a 5-point Calvinist
professor who one day made the statement, "Sinners can't
repent. The Bible nowhere tells them to repent." Instantly my
hand went up. As usual, he would not let me speak. If he had, I
would have cited Acts 17:30: *And the times of this ignorance* God
winked at; but now [Since Jesus came] *commandeth all men
everywhere to repent.*

Generally, those who side with that professor believe once
people are saved they can and will repent. Their error is still
serious for if a sinner cannot repent, and Jesus said unless we do
we will all perish (Luke 13:3, 5), that makes it God's fault that a
person doesn't repent and ends up in hell.

(2) That to teach repentance is essential is to teach salvation by works.

The Scriptures are crystal clear that we are saved by grace through faith and not by works (Ephesians 2:8, 9). Those who teach salvation by works, as all cults do, are saying by doing good works "we earn for ourselves a place in the world to come." My wife and I heard the guide make that statement years ago when we visited the Mormon Tabernacle in Salt Lake City.

As stated above, repentance is the confession and turning from sin because of the conviction and godly sorrow the Holy Spirit has produced in our hearts. Good works are things the sinner is proud of and brags about. Repentance is the opposite. People genuinely repenting, instead of feeling proud, are humbled,

> WHEN THE SOUL WINNER DOES NOT GIVE THE PROPER EMPHASIS TO REPENTANCE, HE IS FAILING
>
> TO LAY A PROPER FOUNDATION FOR HOLY LIVING IN THE NEW CONVERT AND MAY EVEN RESULT IN THE PERSON FAILING TO TRULY GET SAVED.

broken and ashamed. An example of that is seen in the publican getting saved as he, *standing afar off, would not lift up so much as his eyes unto heaven, but smote upon his breast, saying God be merciful to me a sinner.* (Luke 18:13) Again, repentance is inseparable from faith. It is the antithesis of works. The Bible repeatedly contrasts faith and works as the means of salvation. (See Romans 3:27 and Galatians 2:16.)

(3) That a person can receive Jesus as Savior without receiving Him as LORD.

The teaching that a person can be saved by receiving Jesus as Savior without receiving Him as LORD, to a large degree has either eliminated the need for repentance in connection to getting saved, or at least redefined it. It has gained a lot of support in the last half century resulting in bringing many carnal and unsaved people into the church membership and therefore needs to be addressed.

The world's only Savior is the Lord Jesus Christ. To be saved, we must receive Him as He is—the Lord Jesus Christ. The passage in Romans 10, so often used in the familiar "Romans Road" plan presented to the unsaved to show them how to become a Christian, requires a person to confess with his mouth the Lord Jesus (10:9). Not just Jesus, but the LORD Jesus! He came to save us from our sins. (Matthew 1:21) He cannot do that unless we receive Him as Lord. Hearing and believing will result in that *For where your treasure is there will your heart be also.* (Luke 12:34) His name means "Savior." Verses twelve and thirteen both assure the sinner he will be saved if he will repent and receive Jesus as Lord and Savior.

For further proof of God's insistence on holiness among His people, we refer you to the book of Leviticus where, in over 125 places, mankind is indicted for his sin and uncleanness and is told how he can be made pure. The need for such cleanliness and holiness is because God says "I am the LORD" and "I am holy."

Regarding the two lengthy thirteenth and fourteenth chapters of Leviticus (116 verses) that deal with leprosy (a picture of sin), God's purpose there was a health issue, but more than that, He gave them a vivid object lesson stressing how deeply God desires purity, holiness, and cleanness among His people.

It is interesting to note in those chapters that the individual did not look at himself and decide whether or not he had leprosy and was unclean. Instead, repeatedly, the passage states "the priest" shall pronounce him clean or unclean. Jesus is our High Priest. It is his verdict that matters, not our personal opinion. *Every way of a man is right in his own eyes: but the Lord pondereth the hearts.* (Proverbs 21:2)

Before moving to the next section, regarding living out the holiness God requires, remember Paul's instruction to his beloved Timothy to *Keep thyself pure.* (1 Timothy 5:22) He did not say <u>make</u> thyself pure. You cannot. "What can wash away my sins? Nothing but the blood of Jesus." That song states a vital biblical truth. Someone said trying to make your own unsaved heart clean is like trying to mop a dirt floor. While you cannot make yourself clean (*Who can bring a clean thing out of an unclean? Not one.* Job 14:4), we do have the responsibility of utilizing the grace of God to keep ourselves clean.

Whatever keeps us from being men and women of prayer is surely the most destructive thing we face. O those wretched robbers that keep us from accepting the invitation of our High Priest *who is touched with the feelings of our infirmities and is tempted in all points as we are*, who graciously opens the door to His throne room to the only place, yes, and to the only Person from whom we can *obtain mercy, and find grace to help in time of need.* (See Hebrews 4:16-17). We cannot survive without praying. Remember, *The effectual fervent prayer of a righteous man availeth much.* (James 5:16)

Chapter Six

The Basis for Your Convictions

Holy living will characterize our lives only if we have Bible-based convictions that some things are wrong and that we are committed, by the grace of God, to live accordingly. The need for such convictions has increased dramatically in recent years. These words from the famous radio preacher, M.R. DeHaan, founder of the Radio Bible Class tells us why:

> "No man can understand the atonement nor become the recipient of its salvation until he knows something of the awesome holiness of God, and His terrible hatred for sin. God is first of all infinitely righteous, just and holy, so holy, in fact, that even though He is also full of compassion, love, mercy and grace, He cannot and will not allow a single sin to go unpunished. This is basic in the plan of salvation. God is so holy, He hates sin with such a perfect hatred, that He will never permit or allow a single being in His presence without an atonement being made for all of his sin. It is a sad fact, indeed, that we hear so little in these days about the HOLINESS of God. We hear a great deal of his love and compassion, and his mercy, but very, very little of his holiness and justice and righteousness. As a result of this silence concerning God's holiness, we have formed a mean, a low, and a cheap conception of God, while failing to respect His holiness.

"How regrettable that in this age there is so much of this frothy, light and irreverent handling of the holy things of God, making our services a carnival and an entertainment, rather than a place of deep reverential worship of God and the study of His Word. Even in our Christian music today we have sunk too often to the level of jungle jazz. We have lost, I say, much of the reverence for holy things, because of the introduction of much of this shallow entertainment."

--(DeHaan, *The Tabernacle*, 1955).[9]

That was almost sixty years ago. Those of us who have sadly witnessed the death of decency in these intervening years wonder what the courageous preacher would say if he were alive today,

The Bible Alone is the Basis for Correct Convictions

Only God has the right to tell us what is right and what is wrong. He made us. He is the holy, loving, all-knowing, unprejudiced God who is no respecter of persons who, by His very nature, must always do what is right.

Romans 1 makes it clear that every person knows there is a Creator God. Your heart and mind will not allow you to honestly believe in a God who is capricious, arbitrary, or capable of sin. At the same time, your heart and mind, apart from scripture, makes you know you are one day going to die and meet that holy God. Someone has said, of all God's creation, only man is aware that he is going to die and is afraid of it. Scripture supports that when it states, *Forasmuch then as the children are partakers of flesh and blood, he also himself likewise took part of the same* [His Incarnation] *that through death he might destroy him that had the power of death, that is, the devil; And deliver them who through fear of death were all their lifetime subject to bondage.* (Hebrews 2:14-15)

Christ calls men to carry a cross; we call them to have fun in His name.

He calls them to forsake the world; we assure them that if they but accept Jesus the world is their oyster!

He calls them to suffer; but we call them to enjoy all the bourgeois comforts modern civilization affords!

He calls them to holiness; we call them to a cheap and tawdry happiness that would have been rejected with scorn by the least of the Stoic philosophers.
-- (A.W. Tozer)

Let it be known that no man, not a King, not a preacher or a Pope, not a church, not a nation, nor a denomination, has any authority to say authoritatively what is right and what is wrong. That belongs solely to the holy God who created us. While it is never right to go against your conscience, it is not an infallible guide. Conscience, like a computer, acts on what is put into it. Put wrong information in and you get wrong information out. Conscience must be enlightened by the Word of God.

When God created Adam and Eve and placed them in Eden, He gave them one prohibition—not to eat of the tree in the center of the Garden. So what is sin? *Whosoever committeth sin transgresseth also the law: for sin is the transgression of the law.* (1 John 3:4) Whose law? God's law! God said eating what He forbade was sin and the day they ate it they would "surely die." (Genesis 2:17) And they died, not physically that day, but spiritually.

Death does not mean annihilation. It means separation. That day sin severed Adam and Eve from God who alone gives life. (See James 2:26, the body separated from the spirit is dead.) Adam and Eve did eventually die physically also. (Genesis 5:5) God's law prevailed. Our first parents listened to Satan, the great liar and deceiver, and plunged the entire human race into depravity from which we all have suffered. Nothing will change that until hearts are changed by being born again from above and our adopting the Word of God as the rule for our lives. That must be the basis for Christian conduct. But that is not the case with even the church crowd today.

What Determines Most "Christians" Convictions or Lack of Them?

Thou shalt not follow a multitude to do evil. (Exodus 23:2)

But Alas how many do! When a person makes a decision to receive Jesus Christ as their Savior and become a part of a church, they usually adopt the life-style of the people in that congregation. Like produces like. If most of the members of that church attend the three weekly services, the new converts are likely to do the same, if not immediately, in the near future. If the music is traditional they are prone to fit in. If it is contemporary, the same is true. If the church as a whole takes a strong stand against beverage alcohol, nicotine, gambling (playing the lottery), dancing, and dishonoring the Lord's day, if these issues are tactfully and scripturally addressed, the new converts, if they are genuine, are likely to adopt these convictions as their own.

But they must also understand that these standards that the believers are exhibiting are clearly based on the Word of God. If they fail to learn that, if they move to a different congregation, or a new pastor comes who does not adhere to these convictions, they may just as easily mimic the standards (or lack of standards) of the new preacher or congregation. It is a great help in discipling new converts if the believers around them live holy, scriptural standards. At the same time,, the individual needs to see that the truth regarding these standards comes directly from the Holy Bible.

This matter of like produces like is often most easily observed in the matter of dress. Fashion in dress and overall appearance is a big deal in today's American culture. It is usually more evident with the ladies than with men. However, that also is becoming more evident among the men today. Guys fall in with whatever is the coolest and latest style like never before. But the ladies, because of how God made them, are even more style conscious. In over three-score years in the ministry, I have noticed with joy how ladies recently saved notice quickly how the faithful and godly ladies in the congregation dress and quickly adapt. They usually make the adjustment even before they have any teaching on the issue. One special case comes to my mind. This lady gave her heart to the Lord after a Sunday night service and made two major changes the next day—one regarding her wardrobe and the other her work schedule. She was back for church on Wednesday night dressed like the other ladies and back on Sunday for all the services instead of at work where she had been for years.

The point is that in most congregations convictions are more a matter of what is *caught* than what is *taught.* Sadly, this is true regarding what most church people believe as well as how they live. In both cases, the fault can often be laid at the feet of the pastors. The abysmal absence of teaching and preaching on doctrine (the word means truth, teaching) and holy living is a tragedy that is producing a horrible harvest.

We will not dwell long on this point of the failure to preach doctrine today, but a casual visit to your concordance where this word occurs will underscore its vital importance to believers. Regarding the three thousand saved on the birthday of the church, we are told the new converts *continued steadfastly in the apostles' doctrine and fellowship, and in breaking of bread, and in prayers.* (Acts 2:42) When they met, it was not just for food and fellowship. Consider the matter of doctrine also: Romans 6:17 *But God be thanked, that ye were the servants of sin, but ye have obeyed from the heart that form of doctrine which was delivered you.*   When they obeyed from their heart the doctrine Paul had delivered them, those "servants of sin" were set free.

Finally, 1Timothy 6:3-4 ties this matter to the main theme of this book, namely godliness: *If any man teach otherwise, and consent not to wholesome words, even the words of our Lord Jesus Christ, and to* the doctrine which is according to godliness; *he is proud, knowing nothing, but doting about questions and strifes about words, whereof cometh envy, strife, railings, evil surmisings.* Truth—good, Bible based doctrine--will mesh with holy living.

The crying need of the Lord's church today is for a generation of preachers who, not only say they believe the Bible, but pour over it, pray over it, study it from men and books by men who knew it, lived it, and had God's hand on their lives. Such information is readily available free on the internet. That is true of all the sermons of Charles Spurgeon, and the priceless works of Alfred Edersheim, the converted Jew, like his *History of the Old Testament* and *The Life and Times of Jesus the Messiah.*

That's just a fraction of what is out there. But preacher, you need to get some advice about authors you can trust. Read godly men and heed the wisdom and warning of Solomon who wrote *Cease my son, to hear the instruction that causeth to err from the words of knowledge.* (Proverbs 19:27). Learn that popular authors like C.S. Lewis, though a gifted writer was a vile man and a rank heretic. Reading such writers is dangerous. There is plenty of helpful material available. Remember, when you read a worthless book, you wasted your time when you read it, your money when you bought it, dulled your appetite for reading and are now less likely to read a helpful book.

Pastors, you cannot do it all. You must train your leaders to help you. Do as Paul instructed Timothy. *And the things that thou hast heard of me among many witnesses, the same commit thou to faithful men, who shall be able to teach others also.* (2 Timothy 2:2) You are the key. Live in the Book. Live the life. Preach it with a passion. Reproduce yourself spiritually as God helps you.

The need for solid convictions regarding things that are wrong is not only desperately needed, it is scriptural. Many issues are clearly named in the Bible. Count how many sinful things the Apostle Paul named in Ephesians 4 and 5. Other things that are not listed by name are inferred by his statements like the one in Galatians 5:19-21 where he names eighteen different things and then adds, "and such like"—anything akin to these.

That is the answer you need to give to those who say we are not to preach against anything not named in scripture. In the Bible, God gives a number of principles by which, we can determine things that are wrong, though they are not named. These "such like" are largely omitted today. Many prefer to label them "gray areas," which is not a biblical concept. Moral issues are black or white, right or wrong. Yes, there are non-moral things like whether "eating meat" that had been offered to idols (Romans 14 and 1 Corinthians 8) was a sin or not.

In those cases we are admonished to be careful not to offend a "weaker" (untaught) brother, but to defer to him. But eating that meat or not eating it was not a moral issue. Yet, Paul said, if his eating such meat *make my brother to offend, I will eat no flesh while the world standeth.* (1 Corinthians 8:13). Eating the meat was not the problem. Not being concerned for an immature brother was the issue. If that unenlightened, weaker brother thought it was wrong, and Paul, knowing that, ate it anyway, he might cause the untaught brother to do what he believed was sin, causing him to stumble. We are never to do what we believe is wrong, even if it is not. This seems to be a difficult principle to get across. But when it comes to dealing with moral issues, Paul was very serious. Of those sins he stated emphatically, *Of the which I tell you before and I also told you in time past, that they who do such things shall not inherit the kingdom of God.* (Galatians 5:21)

Chapter Seven

Introduction to the Issues

Early in my ministry I learned, almost by accident, that you get people's attention when you deal with the moral issues of the day. Still single and in Bible College, I was preaching morning and night to a rather large group of teens in a youth camp in Oklahoma. I happened to have a box of tracts on various subjects with me. I was staying in the dorm with the guys and reading some of these. Some of them noticed the titles and, at my invitation, they began to read some of them. The ones that caught their eye were those that dealt with the moral issues they were facing.

What they read soon generated a lot of discussion. It spread to the girl's dorm and soon we had a special called session in the afternoon to address the issues. Voluntarily, the majority of the campers came. They were allowed to ask questions. They did not mince words. It was cordial, but they came straight at me. An exchange with one young lady in particular stands out in my memory. She was not one of the current campers, but her father was a pastor of one of the participating churches and she had been to the camp many times in the past.

She had graduated from High School a few weeks earlier. Attractive and popular, she was the Basketball Queen at a large High School that year. During the discussion of some of the issues, she spoke up and said she was a Christian and did those things, but it didn't bother her. She paused and waited for my answer. "All I know to tell you is that there is a good chance you have never been saved, because Hebrews 12 tells us God is a good Father and He, in love, chastises all of his disobedient children."

God used it. She was troubled the remainder of the day and in the service that night. When lights were out later that evening she could not sleep. Finally she roused one of the counselors and asked her to pray with her. Others were awakened. Lights in the girls' area came on. Some still awake in the boys area noticed and wondered what was going on. All the lights were on now. You could hear people talking—praying. It was an awesome evening. More than one full-time Christian worker emerged from that meeting including that Basketball Queen. She showed up at Bible College that fall and in a few years married my roommate and became a pastor's wife.

The next summer, I preached at a number of churches in Arkansas and had a similar experience. Another pastor's daughter whom I talked with after the service, a few nights later roused her dad, told him she didn't think she was saved and prayed with him. She showed up at Bible College that fall and married my other roommate! They have served as missionaries for many years in South America.

As mentioned earlier, the decision to receive Jesus Christ as Savior involves repentance of sin. (1 Thessalonians 1:9) The Holy Spirit convicts a person of their sins (John 16:8-10). As best they know, the penitent must confess and forsake his sin and trust Christ to do what He promised to do and save him. (Romans 10:10)

That same chapter in Romans reminds us, for people to be saved, they must get the gospel from preaching, teaching, or in writing. The sinner is blinded by the god of this world (2 Corinthians 4:3-4). Besides that, unregenerate hearts love darkness (John 3:19) and prefer to continue in their ignorant, lost condition. They do not want to hear the truth, but they must in order to be saved. If we will get it to them, then the Holy Spirit will use that truth to convict them.

Pastor, those who attend your services need to know and have a right to know where you, their Shepherd stands on these issues. You do not have to be mean-spirited, but you must name sin. Paul did. (See 1 Corinthians 6:9-10; Galatians 5:19-21) The world condones sin. They have tried to legitimize all of the Ten Commandments. Even murder. Consider the "legal" murder of millions of babies by abortion!

This applies even to the Christians in your congregation. Multitudes in our midst have never been taught what God has to say on these issues. We are obligated to *Cry aloud, spare not, lift up thy voice like a trumpet, and shew my people their transgression, and the house of Jacob their sins.* (Isaiah 58:1) We will answer to the Chief Shepherd if we fail do so. Pause and ponder this passage from Ezekiel 33:7-8: *So thou, O son of man, I have set thee a watchman unto the house of Israel; therefore thou shalt hear the word at my mouth, and warn them from me. When I say unto the wicked, O wicked man, thou shalt surely die; if thou dost not speak to warn the wicked from his way, that wicked man shall die in his iniquity; but his blood will I require at thine hand.*

A Word to Believers: To my fellow believers, I urge you to support your pastor when he deals scripturally with the issues. You are blessed if you have a pastor who loves his flock enough to warn them against sin, even when it is not popular to do so. You not only need to support him and pray for him, you need to listen to what he is saying, check it out, and if it is biblical, abide by what he says. Remember in the early part of this book we shared with you there is no happiness without holiness. Neither can you have fellowship with the Lord, get your prayers answered, or be a soul winner. Live holy and you can have all of these and you will be in the company of believers, who throughout the history of the church have kept the truth going forth for the next generation.

A Word to Unsaved Hearts: First, let me say that labeling the issues soon to be confronted as sinful will undoubtedly seem to be judgmental, fanatical, or even worse to some. You may be turned off early and say you know Christians and even pastors who do not agree with these positions. Indeed, you may know such people and they may seem to be good Christians in the eyes of many. But please be reminded, the test of truth is what does God's Word say? Please let that and that alone guide you.

Secondly, let me assure you that the God who loves you and gave Jesus, His only begotten Son to save you from your sins, and their penalty, has a plan, that not only makes it possible to pardon you from all your sins, but to change you and cause you to hate what you once loved and love what you once hated. When you are born again, you become a new creature in Christ (2 Corinthians 5:17). You are given a new nature that loves Jesus and hates sin. That faith that saved you will now enable you to have victory over sin. *This is the victory that overcometh the world, even our faith.* (1 John 5:4)

That does not mean you will be sinlessly perfect. That will not happen until the body is redeemed at the second coming of Christ (Romans 8:23), or at our bodily resurrection if we die before He returns. However, it does mean you can live in victory for you have Jesus' promise *There hath no temptation taken you but such as is common to man: but God is faithful, who will not suffer you to be tempted above that ye are able; but will with the temptation also make a way to escape, that ye may be able to bear it.* (1 Corinthians 10:13) You are not left to your own strength for *Ye are of God, little children, and have overcome them: because greater is he that is in you, than he that is in the world.* (1 John 4:4).

You need not be afraid of facing and dealing with sin. Instead, you need to face up to sin, learn what it is, trust Jesus for the victory, and be more afraid of living and dying in sin and suffering its consequences. In the meantime, you will enjoy being a godly Christian for you have another great promise: *For bodily exercise profiteth little: but godliness is profitable unto all things, having promise of the life that now is, and of that which is to come.* (1 Timothy 4:8)

A Personal Note: First, let me say I am grateful for all who will take the time to read the following pages. I am well aware that the positions I am advocating are at odds with today's generation, even church people. I have been told I am a "dinosaur" —something from the distant past that is now extinct. That is not entirely true. As in Elijah's day, there are still a few thousand who have not bowed their knees to Baal (1 Kings 19:18). Be that as it may, I sincerely believe the material I am sharing is, not only scriptural, but is what the Lord's people have stood for historically. May the Holy Spirit give you wisdom and a heart-hunger for holiness as you read.

Chapter Eight

This Matter of Modesty

Ten minutes and two commercials in front of the television ought to convince us that there is a genuine need for some scriptural teaching on this matter of modesty. Our materialistic and decadent society has learned that sex sells and that sexy clothing sells and they have drenched almost every minute of the media with seductive styles. The more skin has been revealed, the more sin has been committed. Hence the flood of fornication, adultery, rape, child molestation, and even murder.

In the classic passage in Proverbs 5-7, the inspired wise man, warned his son about this issue and the many sins connected with it. In that "Anatomy of Adultery "(see section below by that title), he listed a litany of things that contributed to these sins, and also many of its horrific consequences. One thing that father warned his son to avoid was that woman dressed in *the attire of an harlot.* (Proverbs 7:10) The truth from that statement is clear. There is a style of clothing that is associated with that lustful life-style. Christian pastors and parents have a sacred responsibility to God and their children to learn what kind of clothing that is and educate and train their children to dress in a *way which becometh women* [and men] *professing godliness. (*1 Timothy 2:10)

So where do we learn what that is? On all such questions, ask *what saith the scripture?* (Romans 4:3) There is much there relative to this subject. Sadly, few in the pulpits or in the pews have taken the time to seriously search the scriptures to learn what they teach.

A big part of this problem is *the deafening* silence on this subject. There is silence on the side of those who know they should speak against this glaring sin of immodesty today, but there is no silence from the other side. Those who have perverted grace and Christian liberty into a license to sin are very vocal on this issue. Those speakers are supported by a huge chorus of supporters who have been convinced that God's grace somehow makes standards for holy living less on this side of Calvary. Think of that in light of Titus 2:10-11 *For the grace of God that bringeth salvation hath appeared to all men, <u>Teaching us that, denying ungodliness and worldly lusts,</u> we should live soberly, righteously, and godly, in this present world.*

Modesty and The Scriptures

1 Timothy 2:9, 10: *In like manner also, that women adorn themselves in modest apparel, with shamefacedness and sobriety; not with braided hair, or gold, or pearls, or costly array, but (which becometh women professing godliness) with good works.*

We are using the word "modest" as it is commonly understood today with regard to how godly girls and ladies should dress. However, the word translated "modesty" in 1 Timothy 2:9 is the word "cosmos" and means "orderly." In the same verse however, the word that applies to what we are addressing is the word "shamefacedness" in the KJV. We will presently study this word, but first, we need to see the broader picture. We must see that, with regard to this issue of modesty, there is much more involved than merely covering skin. There are other ways for a woman to be seductive than with her clothing or lack of it.

The heart of this issue is the heart. A woman or young girl with a worldly heart, though completely clothed, can find ways to carnally appeal to the opposite sex. Some say they (especially the youth), may do this naively. The prophet Isaiah reprimanded the ladies of his day along this line when he wrote, *Moreover the Lord saith, Because the daughters of Zion are haughty, and walk with stretched forth necks and wanton eyes, walking and mincing as they go, and making a tinkling with their feet: Therefore the Lord will smite with a scab the crown of the head of the daughters of Zion, and the Lord will discover their secret parts.* (Isaiah 3:16-17) The point is that the woman with a heart for holiness is sensitive to her holy God and how He feels about these things. Also, she is conscious of her influence on others around her and desires that her dress will be a testimony for her Lord. There is a drastic difference today in how godly ladies dress from how the worldly dress. The following is an incident that reveals this:

> "One night as another preacher and I, along with our wives and families, were on the street in a large city near our home preaching and passing out gospel tracts during a music festival, when two young women, who were dressed very provocatively, walked by and received the cat-calls and lewd remarks of a couple of young guys. The boys then turned and saw my wife standing there (she is 32), dressed in a modest skirt and top and said, 'Oh, sorry ma'am!' Ladies need to understand, that how they are dressed says a lot about who they are, and determines to some extent how they will be treated."[10]

Now to the word "shamefacedness": The word has no reference to the face. It refers to "the shame or sense of honor that prevents a person from doing something that is wrong. There is the similar word "shamefastness" that would cause a woman to shrink from presenting themselves in such a fashion. This is supposed to hold one back from doing that.

Every godly woman's conscience that has been sensitized by the Holy Spirit, has the Holy Spirit himself living in her. He is there to guide her at all times, especially in times of temptation. And every godly woman, when she has gotten dressed, can stand in front of a full-length mirror, and know if she is dressed like a woman professing godliness should be. Even ungodly women have some sense of this before they sear their consciences to the point God "gives them up to a reprobate mind." (Romans 1:28)

Let me illustrate. Before Jane Fonda made her first movie in which she appeared nude, in an interview she said, in an attempt to do that without feeling uncomfortable, she would go to the beach and sit nude in an effort to try to become comfortable totally exposing herself. When asked if she was still bothered by it, she admitted that she was.

Genesis 2 and 3: From Completely Naked to Properly Clothed by God: This passage teaches us much about what God considers is true modesty. When we are introduced to our first grand-parents, they were fresh from the hand of our holy God and living in a veritable paradise. Scripture tells us *they were both naked, the man and his wife, and were not ashamed.* (Genesis 2:28) Because of sin, it will never be that way again!

Regarding their temptation and disobedience, please notice it was more wicked than it seemed on the surface. The world likes to ridicule this story for many reasons. On this point they like to say, "You mean God pronounced the curse upon them for eating a bite out of an apple?" Please remember, they did it in light of God's clear command, and that they understood and ate it in spite of the fact they did not need it. God had already given them everything they needed. Sin is never something we need!

The Sinner's first reaction to sin: Their eyes were now

open to the fact they were naked and needed to be covered: *The eyes of them both were opened, and they knew that they were naked; and they sewed fig leaves together, and made themselves aprons.* (Genesis 3:7) Question: In verse 11, God asked, "Who told thee that thou wast naked?" The answer is, "No one." Not God nor any person because there was no one else. It is interesting that their first reaction was not anger at the serpent that deceived them or even fear of God. That comes a little later. Nor did they say, "Well, God will forgive us anyhow so it won't matter."

They immediately went from being naked and unashamed (Genesis 2:25), to a keen, condemning feeling of shame. Such a sense of shame is beneficial for sinners. It makes one know sin is shameful and demands a covering. When people can sin without being ashamed, they are ripe for judgment. Jeremiah wrote, *Were they ashamed when they had committed abomination? nay, they were not at all ashamed, neither could they blush: therefore they shall fall among them that fall:* (6:15) It has been said that of all God's creatures, only man can blush—and should.

Adam and Eve's response was an effort to cover their nakedness by making "aprons." (Dr. Adrian Rogers said that was the first mention of mini-skirts.) The word "aprons" simply means "something to gird about." All we know about their "aprons" is their self-made covering was insufficient. God would clothe them sufficiently.

Why do people wear clothes? The unsaved world argues that it is simply a cultural thing that developed over time. They point to heathen tribes that have and some still today who do not wear clothes. They are fond of saying people wear clothes only for decoration and note that some heathen, who do not wear clothes, do paint themselves. The Scriptures in Genesis 3 clearly indicate otherwise. What is the explanation? Again, "What saith the scriptures?" (Romans 4:3) The answer is given in Romans 1 where we read *Wherefore <u>God also gave them up</u> to uncleanness through the lusts of their own hearts, to dishonour their own bodies between themselves: (1:24) For this cause <u>God gave them up</u> unto vile affections: for even their women did change the natural use into that which is against nature: (1:26) And even as they did not like to retain God in their knowledge, <u>God gave them over to a reprobate mind,</u> to do those things which are not convenient. (1:28)*

The Bible teaches that conscience can be "seared" as with a hot iron and no longer signal the warning needed. As these verses indicate, this is done by repeatedly rejecting what a person knows is right. Today's media reveals many in America have done that. They know no shame. Many of the Jews reached that point just before God sent their nation into Babylonian captivity for seventy years. (See Jeremiah 6:15 above and repeated in 8:12.) The point is not the sin had brought them no shame, but that they had killed their consciences by repeatedly going deeper and deeper into sin.

<u>So what was the clothing like that God made for Adam and Eve?</u> *Unto Adam also and to his wife did the Lord God make coats of skins, and clothed them. (Genesis 3:21)*

The word "coats" here is "tunics" in other translations (NKJV) and was basically the same word as "robe" (Exodus 28:4, 31, 34) used to describe the outermost robe God designed for the priests.

Josephus, the Jewish historian about the time of Christ, said it was a long, shirt-like garment that fit close to the body, and reached down to the feet and had sleeves that were tied to the arms. Strong's concordance gives a slightly different word but almost the exact definition for both words.

We should not deduce from this that our clothing today

should be designed exactly like the garments God made for Adam and Eve. However, what is clear is that God supported Adam and Eve's consciousness of their need to be covered. Also, what He made for them covered their nakedness much more completely than what they had made for themselves. God did not intend for fallen man to go naked. I heard a country preacher once say, "If God had intended for Adam and Eve to go naked, He would have haired them over like a mule."

While we are dealing with the matter of modesty and clothing here, we feel constrained to note what God did when He provided the lost and sinful couple with a covering. The Scriptures note the *coats* that God provided were made of skins. Some of His creation surely had to die to provide these skins. At this time Adam and Eve had never seen death. Killing any of these animals that had been like their pets would never have occurred to them. So instead, Adam took leaves from an inanimate, unfeeling tree; God deprived an animal of life that the shame of His creature—man--might be relieved.

These innocent animals did not deserve to die. Instead, Adam and Eve should have been the first to die. They committed the sin. But the covering God provided for them involved the death of an innocent substitute. That prefigured the vicarious death of our Savior centuries later. Those coats of skins, with which Adam and Eve were clothed, is a picture of the robe of Christ's righteousness that He, our innocent Substitute, provided for us by His death for our sin on the Cross.

Their sin cost them dearly, but, as Alfred Edersheim noted,

> "When our first parents left the Garden of Eden, it was not without hope, nor into outer darkness. They carried with them the promise of a Redeemer, the assurance of the final defeat of the great enemy, as well as the Divine institution

of a Sabbath on which to worship, and of the marriage-bond by which to be joined together into families. Thus the foundations of the Christian life, in all its bearings, were laid in Paradise."[11]

Summary: Regarding the matter of modesty, we have learned that sin brought shame without anyone telling the first couple that their nakedness needed to be covered. Their effort to do so was woefully inadequate, so God provided proper covering for them that covered most of their bodies. We have noted in the New Testament, professing Christian women are to dress modestly and that God has built into them something that, unless seared over, causes a woman to blush if she is improperly exposing herself and that this is not a matter of culture. We are now ready to move into the application of the principles we have and are learning from the Scriptures.

Learning Modesty By Applying Bible Principles

God covered Adam and Eve's nakedness. So we need to ask, "What does God consider nakedness?" In the Scriptures, the word *nakedness* occurs 57 times and the word *naked* 47 times. Since God clearly indicated human nakedness needed to be covered, you would think those of us who call Him Father and want to please Him, would want to find out what that involves. My experience has been that very few, even among the clergy, have made such a study. Instead, as indicated earlier, most merely adopt the styles of others around them. Since Paris and Hollywood, rather than God's people, set the styles, we are not surprised that, *as men and seducers wax worse and worse, deceiving and being deceived* (2 Timothy 3:13), that the styles are becoming more and more sensual.

The first time the word *nakedness* occurs in the Bible is in Genesis 9:22. *And Ham, the father of Canaan, saw the nakedness of his father* [Noah], *and told his two brethren without*. This was soon after Noah and his family came out of the ark. He planted a vineyard, grew grapes, made wine, and got drunk from it.

Some say fermentation was not known till after the flood and Noah didn't realize it would make him drunk. Be that as it may, he was drunk and naked in his tent when Ham entered. The curse that followed suggests that Ham looked with evil thoughts. Notice here strong drink and nakedness are linked. They have been ever since. Lustful hearts have long known that if they can get their partner drunk, they can vent their passions. That's why the Scriptures warn *Woe unto him that giveth his neighbour drink, that puttest thy bottle to him, and makest him drunken also, that thou mayest look on their nakedness*! (Habakkuk 2:15)

Getting more to the point of what God calls nakedness and is therefore immodest, we consider the design God dictated for the robes the priests wore in the Old Testament. Notice these two inspired instructions:

Neither shalt thou go up by steps unto mine altar, that thy nakedness be not discovered thereon. (Exodus 20:26)

And thou shalt make them linen breeches to cover their nakedness [bare flesh, marginal reading]*; from the loins even unto the thighs they shall reach.* (Exodus 28:42)

That first verse made it clear that, since the priests wore robes, they were not to build an altar high where, when the priest went up the steps, it would be possible for others to look up his robe.

The second passage is very specific, teaching us that God's description of nakedness is the uncovering of the *thighs*. The thigh is that part of the human anatomy that reaches from the loins to the knees.

Uncovering the leg and the thigh and calling it shameful nakedness is repeated again in Isaiah 47:2-3: *Take the millstones, and grind meal: uncover thy locks, make bare the leg, uncover the thigh, pass over the rivers. Thy nakedness shall be uncovered, yea, thy shame shall be seen: I will take vengeance, and I will not meet thee as a man.* The passage deals with the time when God would deal with Israel's enemy, Babylon.

In this day of cafeteria style Christianity, where people pick what they want and leave the rest, even those who know these verses are here are prone to ignore them. We do not have the right to do that or to say that it is not for us for we are not under Law but under grace. In an effort to help wives with unsaved husbands win them to Christ, Peter went back to the days of Abraham and Sarah and urged the Christian wives to emulate Sarah and other holy women like her in dress and submission. Also, the apostle Paul pointed to the sins of God's people in the wilderness-- when they made and worshipped a golden calf. Scripture informs us the Jews were naked *for Aaron had made them naked unto their shame among their enemies.* (Exodus 32:25) The Bible tells us what it cost them and then he reminded New Testament believers *Now all these things happened unto them for examples: and <u>they are written for our admonition</u>, upon whom the ends of the world are come.* (1 Corinthians 10:11)

Like all of God's truth, we ignore it at our peril. And pastors, let me remind us, we promised to preach the "<u>whole</u> counsel of God." Brethren, it is not enough to say we are for modesty. We must define it and teach our flocks the Scriptures that spell it out. That is a serious part of the under shepherds' responsibility. Your people have a right to know where their shepherd stands on the issues. And they expect you to be more conservative than they are. You do not have to try to be. Just teach your people and live it before them.

Before listing various kinds of dress that would violate what we have learned above, let us briefly review and make another observation.

Review: When the first humans sinned, from a sense of shame they realized they were naked and needed to be covered. God rejected their self-made covering as insufficient and provided coats of skins that covered them from their necks to below the knees. This covering applied to both the man and the woman.

Observation: Genesis 35 records Jacob's return to Bethel, the place where he first met his Lord. The passage reveals there was a great revival in his family at this time. Obeying God's command to return to Bethel with his family, *Jacob said unto his household, and to all that were with him, Put away the strange gods that are among you, and be clean, and change your garments. And let us arise, and go up to Bethel; and I will make there an altar unto God, who answered me in the day of my distress, and was with me in the way which I went.* (Genesis 35:2-3)

For the first time, Jacob stepped up and became the loving leader in his own home. He told them what they must do and they obeyed him. We would have an entirely different story in the Old Testament history if he had not and they had not.

In noting his insistence that they change their garments, we wonder if what had happened to Dinah, his teen-age daughter in the previous chapter, was not related to this. Jacob had moved his family into an area where he should not have been. Contrary to the pilgrim life he was to live, he had bought land, built a house, and settled down short of where God told him to go. Then we read *And Dinah the daughter of Leah, which she bare unto Jacob, went out to see the daughters of the land.*

Did the way Dinah was dressed contribute to what

happened to her? It does in myriads of cases every day. The wise man, Solomon, warned his son to avoid certain women. One of their identifying marks was their dress—"the attire of a harlot." (Proverbs 7:10) It doesn't always have to be a dress that is very revealing. When the police in our area were trying to catch a rapist, they dressed a female officer, not in shorts and a halter top, but in faded, sloppy jeans, and a man's shirt. She gave the appearance that she had been handled before and didn't care. It worked. They caught the culprit. Remember, the word "modesty" in 1Timothy 2:9 means properly arranged. She wasn't.

The Matter of Mixed Swimming

"It used to be when a woman went swimming, she looked like Mother Hubbard. Now she looks like Mother Hubbard's Cupboard!"

Putting the girls and boys together in the same pool is popular today at church camps, Christian colleges, and church outings. Many claim they are fundamental, Bible-believing people. Many of these same groups used to speak out against this, prompting the question, "Were we right then, or are we right now?"

Let's be honest. There are no swimsuits on the market today that meet what the Bible clearly teaches on this subject of modesty. Please seriously consider what is shared below regarding both men and women. I am well aware that much of this will be going against popular opinion and practice. That is not a new experience for me. I pastored in Miami, FL for three years and have lived in Virginian Beach for the past forty-nine years. Beaches are synonymous with these cities.

When talking with Christians who participate in mixed swimming, I have not had people try to defend it from the Scriptures. The usual reply is similar to what the Youth for Christ director in Miami said to me when I told him our young people would not be going to the beach party. He said, "I know what you are saying and I agree, but it just a little matter and not worth arguing over." Just a "little matter?" Who are we to decide that? And I seem to recall that Solomon wrote, that it is the "<u>little</u> foxes the spoil the vines," rendering them fruitless. (Song of Solomon 2:15) Maybe that explains the embarrassingly barren altars and empty spiritual cribs in our churches. "Just a little matter?" That's more of that "Cafeteria Christianity" where you take what you like and leave the rest. We need Bible Christianity and to be willing to follow what God likes, instead of following the crowd and our own selfish, fleshly desires.

In a showdown experience while I was still in my teens, I told the Lord if He would show me what is right as taught in His Word, by His grace I would try to live by it. The person who does otherwise will forfeit having God's hand on his life. The only way to explain the awesome success of the New Testament Church is that they were a praying people with the power of the Holy Spirit on their lives. Acts 5:32 explains we have His power only if we obey Him. *And we are his witnesses of these things; and so is also the Holy Ghost, whom God hath given to them that <u>obey</u> him.*

But back to the bathing suits: The styles really began to change in the late '20's and early 30's, right after the great depression. A person could be arrested on Atlantic Beach in New Jersey for being topless. We are not talking about the ladies. They wouldn't have dared try that back then. This was men. They rebelled against the law. Tops were made that pushed the limits. By 1935 most public beaches had admitted defeat and manufactures quickly made and marketed the now "legal" topless swim suits for men. The women soon were demanding to be allowed to expose more skin. Since then our generation has proven "MORE SKIN = MORE SIN." Does dealing with this sound prudish to you? Or does the harvest of broken homes, our kids gone wild, and the flood of fornication resulting in almost half of the babies born in USA today being illegitimate, does that bother you more?

Concluding this section, for anyone who thinks the nearly nude swimwear of both men and women, does not contribute to the flood to immorality in our nation today, consider this: While pastoring in Miami fifty years ago, I read that 85% of women's swim suits never got in the water. So why are they out there? And why are the Florida Beaches so overcrowded by college students during Spring break. Filthy films like "Girls Gone Wild" tell the sordid story.

Men and Modesty

It is widely believed that men are more attracted to the opposite sex by sight while women are more sensitive to touch. However, that does not mean men should not be careful about how they dress.

If you need evidence that the weaker sex is also attracted by sight, consider the case of Joseph and Potiphar's wife. (Genesis chapter 39) Joseph "was á goodly person and well favored." The New King James translates it "Joseph was handsome in form and appearance." His body was well-formed and his face handsome. Next, scripture tell us "that his master's wife cast her eyes upon Joseph; and she said, Lie with me." (39:7)

The fashion world tells us women dress to attract men while men dress to gain status. To whatever degree that is true, those are general rules and do not preclude the fact women are also attracted by sight and therefore men need to dress in a way they are not unduly causing a problem.

Dr. Mark Minick, a pastor in Greenville, SC and professor at Bob Jones University, related a story of young single girl who worked in the office with his wife. He said during some of the

Olympic Games, she would come to work just "oozing" over the body of a diver named Greg Louganis, winner of multiple gold medals.

On a more personal note, two of my daughters were in Bible College when the change was made from men wearing trousers on the basketball court to the, traditional uniforms. They were not accustomed to that. When I asked them if it bothered them, they said it did. I suggest to you that Christian men on the court in those uniforms for the first time were also bothered. In High School the first time I went on the floor dressed that way it bothered me. The same was true the first time I went to a public swimming pool.

There is also another important reason why men should dress modestly. That is the matter of homosexuality where men are attacked to men. Fellows, those days when we used to meet and play basketball when one team would be "shirts" and the other "skins" should be forever over for those of us who are the ambassadors of King Jesus. The same applies to mixed swimming.

Don't try to dodge the issue. One pastor who was in the motel swimming pool, along with other men and women at one of the National Association meetings of our churches told some of us he did not believe in mixed swimming. He said he was only getting his exercise.

For Ladies to Consider Regarding Modesty

Ladies, what has been said to the men, needs to be said to you even more. Men are strongly attracted to you by sight. Jesus said, *That whosoever looketh on a woman to lust after her hath committed adultery with her already in his heart.* (Matthew 5:28) If you are not properly dressed, you are an accomplice to the sin. Don't try to pass the blame entirely to the man by saying, "He's just got a dirty mind." It is normal for men to be attracted by suggestive exposure. This was true with one of the most righteous men in the Bible.

Consider Job. The Bible says *he was perfect and upright, and one that feared God, and eschewed evil.* (Job 1:1) We often speak of the patience of Job, but scripture stresses his righteousness more. Yet, this godly man said *I made a covenant with mine eyes; why then should I think upon a maid?* (Job 31:1) Every man ought to make such a covenant with his eyes. There will still be a battle that he will win only with the help of the Holy Spirit. And ladies, you can help.

A more familiar case is the story of David and his sin with Bathsheba. I am confident my readers are familiar with that story as recorded in 2 Samuel 11. David was no longer a youth. He had fought and won many battles and was now the most powerful ruler in the world. But he was not on his guard that night or where he should have been. From the flat roof of his palace *he saw a woman washing herself; and the woman was very beautiful to look upon.* (2 Samuel 11:2) That night David--the only man ever described as *a man after his* [God's] *own heart,"* (1 Samuel 13:14) lost the battle of his life to the flesh.

We ask, "Why David?" Like Adam and Eve in Eden, David had no need for that woman. He was a married man. And Bathsheba was married to another man! Not just any man, but Uriah. One of David's special and most devoted soldiers—one of his illustrious *mighty men.* (2 Samuel 23:39)

Here was a godly man, succumbing to the flesh, lured only by what he saw. He did not know her, apparently had never talked with her, but followed the flesh even after he was told she was the wife of Uriah! He was guilty! He had to answer to God for his sin. But Bathsheba was not innocent. If David could see her, she could see him. David didn't know who she was, but she is bound to have known who lived in that palace. At the worst, she purposely exposed herself. At best she did what every normal woman knows she should not do--expose herself where others' eyes could see her. Like David, she also paid a high price for her sin. She lost a devoted and apparently godly husband as well as her baby.

To the Christian ladies reading this, take heed. Even if you have a Christian husband, you need to realize he is also a man. You trust him, but you need to help him also. Like many other men, he is going to be among other women on his job. Some, usually the majority of them, are not saved. If they are in step with the styles of today, they will usually be dressed provocatively. He is not only likely to be exposed to such sights, but he is also likely to hear others making unsavory comments. He loves you and deep down, never plans to betray his wedding vows. The Holy Spirit is there to help him. No one has to yield to these temptations. But as Jesus said to Peter, *the spirit is indeed willing, but the flesh is weak.* (Matthew 26:41) Ladies, please wise up. Don't wait until you get a phone call in the middle of the night.

How Sexual Temptation Works

To deal with the kind of temptation we are discussing, it helps to understand how the process works. James 1:13-15 is an excellent passage on the subject.

Let no man say when he is tempted, I am tempted of God: for God cannot be tempted with evil, neither tempteth he any man But: every man is tempted, when he is drawn away of his own lust, and enticed; Then when lust hath conceived, it bringeth forth sin: and sin, when it is finished, bringeth forth death.

God tests us to strengthen us, but He never tempts us to cause us to stumble. So we can't blame Him. Nor can we say, as many do, "The Devil made me do it." We must face the reality that the problem is our own lustful, fallen flesh. The word "lusts" refers to our wrong desires. "Drawn away" refers to the practice of baiting a trap to lure animals into it. Something desired that they want and think will be pleasant draws them. When they indulge those desires, they find it also brings pain and death.

Lest we fall for Satan's lies when he tells us God withholds everything that is good from us, we need to realize temptation involves the wholesome, God-given desires, but seeks to satisfy them in the wrong way. When God created Adam and Eve, He gave them the desire for physical intimacy. He told them to have children. He provided a holy way for those desires to be satisfied within the boundaries of holy matrimony.

One of several words for sin in scripture is the word "trespass." We often see that on signs to tell us we are not to enter that property. Sin is when we "trespass" and, to satisfy those God-given desires, go over those holy boundaries God has set. He placed them there for our own good. *For this is the love of God, that we keep his commandments: and his commandments are not grievous.* (1 John 5:3) God's Law is *the perfect law of liberty* (James 1:25), not a law of bondage.

Returning to the passage in James 1, notice the word "enticed." This is a fishing term, similar to "drawn away." Temptation is when the bait has gotten the attention and stimulated the desires of the one being tempted. This happened when David "<u>saw</u>" Bathsheba bathing. It could have ended there. He <u>should </u>have turned away. But he didn't. Sin is a process and next David began to make plans. He "<u>sent</u>" for her. She came. He was now on very dangerous ground. But it could still have ended there. But again, it didn't. He was now "enticed" and once enticed, it is seldom ended there. The only thing remaining was for her to be willing. She was and now *"lust hath conceived."* Now it is too late. Once sin has been conceived, the unwanted but deserved consequences will follow. Sin has been committed and its inevitable wages will be paid. There will be death.

Warnings: In today's world, the above process is often begun by men looking at seductive pictures in magazines, movies, or more commonly now, on TV and the internet. Seductive talk is also available. Men know this and when they choose to access such websites and phone numbers, they have usually already made plans or are willing to do so.

While men are more prone to take this route, women are increasingly doing the same. Since this material is so easily available and in such private environments of our homes or motels, professing and/or weak and backslidden believers are often tempted to log on or dial up. A pastor told me yesterday that he recently read that those who use such sites in motels and hotels the most are religious organizations that have their conventions there. That sounds preposterous, but to whatever degree it is true, that explains why the flocks continue to be shocked by news their shepherd is forced to resign (or should be) due to this sin of adultery. Almost every case this writer can think of where a preacher has gone bad, these avenues into adultery are involved. The same is true for preachers' wives.

Apologies are due from the Preachers: *His watchmen are blind: they are all ignorant, they are all dumb dogs, they cannot bark; sleeping, lying down, loving to slumber.* (Isaiah 56:10)

Isaiah, the prince of the prophets, and others (cf. Ezekiel 3), blamed those who should be warning people of sin and its consequences for much of the corruption of their day. Every person knows there is a God to whom they must give an account (Romans 1). They *shew the work of the law written in their hearts and their conscience*. (Romans 2:15) Yet, a merciful and just God has sent His servants to every generation, ordained and qualified, to preach His gospel and cry out against sin. Those who are faithful to do so are often persecuted. To the others, God says *thou, O son of man, I have set thee a watchman unto the house of Israel; therefore thou shalt hear the word at my mouth, and warn them from me.* (Ezekiel 33:7)

It is still rather common for preachers to preach against sin and mention modesty. The problem is they are afraid to define sin. They don't want to be labeled a "legalist," which they probably would be if they were to do so. Also, if the truth were known, in many cases they are fearful of offending their people, resulting in losing members, money, and being seen as so "controversial" they could not get recommended to another church if they struck out where they were. Consequently, while few dare name and define sin, the cry from the crowd of cowards is deafening!

We ask, should the weeping prophet Jeremiah be labeled a "legalist" for writing *Will ye steal, murder, and commit adultery, and swear falsely, and burn incense unto Baal, and walk after other gods whom ye know not, And come and stand before me in this house, which is called by my name, and say, We are delivered to do all these abominations?* Or how about *Moses, the man of God* who wrote *And thou shalt not let any of thy seed pass through the fire to Molech, neither shalt thou profane the name of thy God: I am the LORD:* He was crying out against the sins of his day and naming them. If that is legalism, count me in!

Coming to the New Testament, read again the words of the apostle Paul, the man whom God used to write approximately half of it. Make a list of the sins he lists in such passages as Ephesians 4-5 and Galatians 5 where he wrote, *Now the works of the flesh are manifest, which are these; Adultery, fornication, uncleanness, lasciviousness, idolatry, witchcraft, hatred, variance, emulations, wrath, strife, seditions, heresies, envyings, murders, drunkenness, revellings, and such like: of the which I tell you before, as I have also told you in time past, that they which do such things shall not inherit the kingdom of God.* After counting the seventeen, don't miss the addition <u>"and such like."</u>

Apply that to those things the perverters of Christian liberty like to call "gray areas"—a category not found in scripture.

Apologies from pastors for their failure to preach against and name the sins of our generation are seldom given. They are therefore betraying the trust God has given them, resulting in the people in the pew being left to learn for themselves—often the hard way—how what God says is sin and how serious are its consequences.

So What Is Modest and What Is Not?

The Pastor is not to go to the ladies closets and inspect each item. As we shall discuss soon, the parents have some definite authority and responsibility to do that for their children. Additionally, the fathers and husbands, as God's designated heads of the home, have much responsibility regarding how the wives and children are dressed. What measures up to the principles given in the Scriptures determines what is modest and what it is not. Husbands have the responsibility to learn what those are and see to it that they are adhered to by those under his roof. In an effort to try to help, in this section, we will begin with some general principles and then move to applying these to more specifics. We begin with the ladies.

They are the ones addressed most on this issue. We see this in 1 Timothy 2:9-10 where there are three principles given guiding how a godly woman ought to dress.

In like manner also, that women adorn themselves in modest apparel, with shamefacedness and sobriety; not with broided hair, or gold, or pearls, or costly array.

- **Modesty**
- **Propriety**
- **Femininity**

Modesty: As we noted earlier, this word in the original language refers, not to what we associate with the word modesty, but means to be dressed orderly. The godly lady, because she has been bought with a price and belongs to Jesus, is *therefore* [to] *glorify God in* [her] *body and in* [her] *spirit, which are God's.* (1 Corinthians 6:20)

MODESTY IS MORE THAN MERELY COVERING SKIN.

She is not to be sloppy and disarranged, but neat and well-kept. There is much in today's styles that violates this. Faded and ragged jeans are popular with the world's crowd, but my sister in Christ, Jesus said we are not of this world (John 15:19). We are His children and represent Him. If we prefer to be a friend of this world, Jesus' half-brother, James tells us that *the friendship of the world is enmity with God* (and*) whosoever therefore will be a friend of the world is the enemy of God.* (James 4:4) So whose friend do you want to be?

It is one thing for a woman to be dressed in ragged clothes if she is poor and destitute. It is another thing for her to choose to dress that way to be a part of the "in" crowd that lives a lifestyle of abandon. It is natural for a woman to want to look as pretty as she can. She has to go against God-given inhibitions to intentionally dress disorderly.

Propriety: This should need very little explanation. The lady of the house should dress differently when doing housework, or working in the yard. However, such activities are not to be occasions for immodest or suggestive dress. When she is going to church or some formal occasion, she should wear the best she has, but not to the point she is hoping to catch the eyes of others, either men or women, by going to the extreme. A good policy for all of us on dressing for church is to call no attention to ourselves so we can call all attention to Jesus. Pastors, that is a good rule for us also. The preacher dressed in bib overalls or a tuxedo would be a distraction in most services. The same applies to hair, hats, footwear and all in between.

Femininity: The verses above give good guidelines for _women_ _professing godliness._ Christian ladies are to dress in such a way that no one has any difficulty recognizing that she is a woman and not a man. Her hair as well as her clothing should help make that distinction. _Doth not even nature itself teach you, that, if a man have long hair, it is a shame unto him?_. How long is long and how short is short need not become a sticking point. Hair styles change. Ladies, what might be considered long at one time might be too short. The principle is to be distinguished from the normal hair style of the men at that time, ignoring the men who, to their shame, have adopted feminine hair styles and also much of their dress styles.

I would be derelict in my duty on this point to evade Moses' instructions as recorded in Deuteronomy 22:5: _The woman shall not wear that which pertaineth unto a man, neither shall a man put on a woman's garment: for all that do so are abomination unto the Lord thy God._

The issue at hand is women dressing like a woman and not a man. The men are also addressed and told they are not to wear women's garments. The latter is not very common, though it is becoming more visible with the homosexual and transgender upsurge.

For the ladies, the question arises about wearing pants. A generation ago, most churches that would be considered fundamental, Bible believing congregations would have said you should not. If a woman attended one of those churches in pants, she would probably have felt out of place. Today, the opposite is true. Again, the question, were we wrong then or are we wrong now? This is not a mere academic question. There is much to be considered. You must consider what God's Word has to say on the issue, get the most godly counsel you can find, and make sure your motive is to bring glory to our Lord. Then be prepared to face Him with your decision.

Some Specifics About What Is and is Not Modest

Every Christian lady is obligated to dress in accordance with the Bible teachings on this subject. She must therefore take an honest look at each garment she wears and make a decision as to whether or not it meets the guidelines of our holy God.   Is it modest or is it not? The following is this writer's attempt to help you.

Remember, we are using the word "modest" in the sense in which it is understood today, meaning if it is revealing or calling attention to parts of your body that could unduly pose temptation for the opposite sex, it is immodest. As stated earlier, Pastors cannot inspect the wardrobes of all the ladies in his flock. However, if he is a man of God and evidences the fact that he is a serious student of the Scriptures, each of those ladies should value and even desire his opinion. Remember, *Where no counsel is, the people fall. But in the multitude of counselors there is safety.* (Proverbs 11:14) Of course that means the counsel of the godly for the opening verse of the Psalms warns us not to *walk in the counsel of the ungodly.* If you listen to them on this subject, you know—indeed you see all around you--what you will get!

Perhaps I should share some things from my ministry that might suggest I may have something to offer on this subject. My ministry stretches back over sixty years, including six years in good Christian colleges, forty years of pastoring churches (averaging over a thousand in attendance for the last 25 years), writing the Adult Sunday School quarterly for our denomination for seventeen years and publishing *The Gist*, a magazine for

Pastors for thirty years. In addition, our church kept me on the air live five days a week for over 22 years, preaching daily to approximately twenty thousand people a day (Arbitron ratings), ending each day with an invitation to listeners to call me. As you might surmise, I dealt with about every issue imaginable.

My ministry kept me in touch with many young people from our Christian School (average enrollment over four hundred for most of those years) as well as those in our church. My wife and I have five daughters (and one son) and have seven grown grand-daughters. Suffice to say, their questions on these issues have been the same as yours. I pray the following will be helpful in your decisions. So here are some of my gleanings.

A close friend, Evangelist Guy Owens was the first to share the following with me. He noted (and the Scriptures back it up), that your attire is immodest when it is:

- **Too tight**
- **Too thin**
- **Too short or**
- **Too low at the top**

Recently I read scores of letters from fundamental, Christian men who responded to a pastor's questionnaire on what they considered to be immodest dress for the ladies and their reactions to it. Their candid comments concerned mostly the ladies in their churches. Here are some of those comments.

They would specifically state the problem and often blame the preachers whose "convictions" were "only as deep as the crowd allowed and decried the fact that often the pastors' family was not a good model of modesty.

One mentioned "modesty is more than merely covering skin." He mentioned slit skirts that he labeled "peek-a-boo" skirts.

Regarding garments that are too thin, one commented, "If a woman is standing where the light can shine through her skirt, though she may be covered with a garment, it is so transparent, everything is revealed." Another applied it to sheer blouses.

Much was said about the garments being too tight. Here are a couple of them: "You don't even need to see skin; they provide all the curves." Another said: "I would say the number one problem is any garment that is form fitting, be it jeans, pants, skirt, dress, and shirt, whatever. Anything that is tight, no matter how long it is, leaves nothing to the imagination, and that defeats the whole purpose of covering the skin in the first place!"

A REVEALING TEST FOR LADIES

WHERE DO MEN'S EYES GO FIRST WHEN THEY ARE LOOKING AT YOU?

IF IT IS NOT YOUR FACE, YOU NEED HELP.

As a real potential for lust they mentioned short skirts, tight skirts, slit skirts, long skirts with slits to the knees, sleeveless blouses, low cut blouses, tight blouses, sheer blouses, V-neck T-shirts, form-fitting dresses, jeans, pants, and shorts.

The men often admitted they had problems even at church regarding these things.

One said, it really bothered him that, after having to face so much of this out in the world all week, he had to face it even at church.

The cleavage at the top, so much in vogue in the world's styles today, and so common in churches, was considered a real problem. My son, who was attending a large fundamental church at the time, said the pastor one Sunday, asked how many men there had been embarrassed over this. He said over a hundred said they had. It often poses a special problem for the ushers when they are receiving the offering.

> **Repeatedly, these men said they wrestled with these problems and urged the ladies to help. Some who had been down those wrong roads in the past were especially troubled by what they faced even at church. Several said they felt the ladies did not realize what a serious problem this is.**

The statement above is referring to men's eyes being drawn to cleavage because of plunging necklines. Ads for tight-fitting jeans focus on another part of the body. The pictures of women in jeans on the billboards almost always show the view from the rear. You don't see many pretty faces today. That doesn't seem to be where photographers or the lustful eyes of most men are looking. The sexual implication that is revealed in these ads should give ladies added reason to question whether they should wear such garments. Also, such attire raises the question discussed above regarding women wearing men's garments. Deuteronomy 22:5 that says, *the woman shall not wear that which pertaineth unto a man, neither shall a man put on a woman's garment: for all that do so are abomination unto the Lord thy God.*

Yes, some jeans/pants are now designed for women, but many, especially the younger women, are prone to wear either. Also, as everyone knows, and as the emblems on every restroom door worldwide shows, pants indicate which is for men and dresses indicate which is for women. Something else we all know is that when the style of women changed from their wearing dresses for centuries to wearing pants, the change was not brought about by godly Christian women. Moreover, no one is likely to argue that the switch from dresses to pants was the result of careful study of God's Word on the issue and much prayer from yielded hearts. As indicated earlier, most follow the crowd, not the Scriptures.

Only godly leaders with biblical convictions and hearts hungry for holiness will be blessed by our Holy God. The carnal crowd is filling their nets, but when they are brought to shore and sorted out under the eyes of the eternal Judge, the results are going to be disappointing. (Matthew 13:47-48. See Also 2 Corinthians 3:12-15) Where can we get godly leaders? And also, where are the church leaders with correct convictions and enough courage to say we are no longer going to spend God's money purchasing religious literature that promotes these things by putting such books into the hands of our people –especially our youth—to tilt them more toward the world. Someone is going to have to answer for that.

One more observation needs to be made before leaving this topic: Suggestive messages written on the clothes, especially where they are calling attention to certain parts of the body, are obviously off limits. Suggestive words and those with double meanings are also taboo, not only printed on their clothing, but neither are they to be tattooed on their skin. Inspired by God, Moses wrote in Leviticus 19:28: *You shall not make any cuttings in your flesh for the dead, nor tattoo any marks on you: I am the Lord.* (New King James Version) Christian, let me ask you the question the Apostle Paul asked the carnal Corinthian Christians, *What? know ye not that your body is the temple of the Holy Ghost which is in you, which ye have of God, and ye are not your own?*

We know what that price was, don't we? The precious blood of Jesus shed to make possible the forgiveness of our sins. We know something else also. We know this fad did not come from God's people, but from the worldly crowd. Those who participate in this make it clear which side they want to emulate and impress.

Knowing the above goes against so much that is accepted behavior today, I ask the ladies and the men also, to the degree this material applies to you, to consider these matters seriously and prayerfully. My purpose is to help holiness again be clearly evident in our churches and even in the marketplace. Remember, the church is the window through which the world sees who Jesus is and what Christianity is. God's Word describes this world as a *wicked and adulterous generation* (Matthew 16:4) whose *eyes are full of adultery*. (2 Peter 2:14)

Surely we cannot look seriously upon the horrible harvest this sin is causing and not be moved with compassion. Masses of broken hearted husbands, weeping wives, crying children, and crippled churches, ought to put us on our knees begging God to help us do what we can to change this. And you can add to that the tragic picture of widespread domestic violence and even murders and numerous suicides this sin is spawning, not to mention what it is doing to the very fabric of our society as a nation. Most of all, we must face the reality that those involved in this lifestyle are in the fast-lane on the highway to hell. The Bible makes this clear in such passages as Proverbs 5:5, 7:27, 1 Corinthians 6:9, and Revelation 21:8.

Grand-Motherly Advise to Mothers About Their Children

Train your daughters to dress modestly when they are very young. If you wait until they're teens, you have probably lost the battle. It may be a drawn-out battle, but it is winnable. Don't give them ill-clad dolls like Barbie. Grand-mother can tell you why.

Chapter Nine

An Anatomy Of Adultery
Inspired information To Avoid it
Proverbs 5-7

The purpose for dealing with the sin of immodesty is to help prevent the awful sin of adultery. In the seventh of the Ten Commandments, God said *Thou shalt not commit adultery.* (Exodus 20:14) There is a progression in how the commandments are arranged. The first deals with the worst of sins, dishonoring God, His name, His day, etc. Secondly, is the dishonoring of parents. Those are very serious sins. Then comes how we treat others.

Number six tells us the worst thing we can do to another person is to murder them. Next to that, the worse thing is to commit adultery with them. One of the gravest inversions of morality in today's society to see this sin glamorized, flaunted, and promoted. It has been relabeled, but its tragic consequences have not changed nor its price reduced. The wages of this sin and all sin is still death. (Romans 6:23)

In order to help prevent the sin of adultery, long ago God inspired King Solomon to teach his son how to avoid it. The advice this wise-man gave his son has been graciously preserved for us to help us teach our children these important lessons. The subject is completely covered from the first contact to the immoral act itself and the eternal as well as the earthly consequences are listed.

Urging his son to listen carefully, Solomon began by addressing this alluring temptation by saying, *The lips of a strange woman* [one not his wife] *drop as a honeycomb and her mouth is smoother than oil. But her end is bitter as wormwood, sharp as a two-edged sword. Her feet go down to death"* her *steps take hold on hell.* (Proverbs 5:3-5)

This is where we should begin in dealing with this sin. Today's sex education in public schools only excites and encourages this sin. Snickers and smirks from the students are common in such classes. Discussions in church circles with young people are usually more discreet, but often stop short of conveying what is given to us in Proverbs.

As a writer of literature for our denomination for seventeen years, I often attended conferences for writers. At one of those, I questioned what was being published for our youth on the subject. I called attention to a recent article where they were told to avoid such sin for fear they might contract disease or produce an illegitimate child.

Referencing the passage above, I noted, if we are to address this subject at all (which I consider inappropriate in most settings. It should be done in the home.), we ought to sound the warning that the Bible does and tell them this sin leads to hell! That usually wipes away the smirks and the jokes.

Lured by her lips: Next, Solomon continued his warning to his son by addressing the lips of the "strange woman." He cautions him about her kisses (7:13) and her flattery (6:24, 7:21) He said, *"with the flattering of her lips she forced him...knoweth not that it is for his life.* (Proverbs 7:21-23)

This is a two-way street. If the other party begins to say things like "I wish I had a husband (or wife) like you" (compare 7:15), you are headed for trouble. If such talk comes from the other party, do what Joseph did when Potiphar's wife tried to seduce him. "He left his garment in her hand, and fled, and got him out." (Genesis 39:12) All of us need to make a covenant that we will never be guilty of such talk and, as best we can, never allow ourselves to be in a situation where someone might feel free to say this to you or you to them.

Flattery usually precedes and leads to more intimate contact, namely kisses. Meant to express love, in the wrong situation, they stir unholy, fleshly lusts. My teenage Sunday School teacher gave the best advice I have ever heard when she told us, "Young people, save your kisses for the one you are going to marry." Not just until you are engaged, but until you are married. Kissing leads to fondling and you are then into the "enticement" spoken of in James 1:14. After that, it is seldom stopped until it is too late.

Lured by her Beauty and her eyes: Scripture records that Bathsheba was <u>very beautiful </u>to look upon. (2 Samuel 11:2) The word for beauty there is, according to Strong's concordance, used in "the widest sense." In short, she was a knockout! That was what drew David into the worst thing that ever happened in his life. John speaks of "the lust of the eyes" as being one of the three great avenues of temptation (1 John 2:16). Jesus said *Whosoever looketh on a woman to lust after her hath committed adultery with her already in his heart.* (Matthew 5:28)

As stated below, God's most beautiful creation is the woman. But, after Adam and Eve's sin, God properly covered both of them. He never intended for a woman to uncover herself to anyone other than her husband. Neither did He intend for any man to look upon an exposed woman that was not his wife. Bathsheba's beauty was the bait that hooked David that awful evening. She was very beautiful, but all that beauty was on the outside, and like all God's gifts, when used in the wrong way is sinful. It is not wrong for a woman to make herself as nice looking as she can. However, the often quoted idea that "If you've got it, flaunt it" is a lie and will cost you more than you will want to pay.

Outward beauty is a jewel only if accompanied with inward beauty. Otherwise, all such beauty is vain.   (Proverbs 31:30)

We are not surprised that the Bible warns men regarding being lured into sin by a woman's beauty. But the warning about being reeled in with her eyes sounds unreal. Yet we are cautioned, "Neither let her take thee with her eyelids." (Proverbs 6:25) While that may sound strange to men, it will not to the ladies. Every woman (and most men) knows that there are other ways of being seductive than simply by the way a woman dresses. Flirting is part of the "come on" and the eyes play a vital part in that. When I was growing up, I heard a song that said, "Her lips tell me No, No, but there's Yes, Yes in her eyes." Ladies, you need to avoid such action and fellows, if they don't, you need to follow Joseph and get yourself out!

Watching a Fool Fall into this Sin

In the closing verses of Proverbs 7, Solomon pictures standing at a window watching a young man as he ignores all kinds of warnings and walks right into this serious sin. We will follow him and underline those things the wise man noted.

First, he went to the wrong section of town--to her corner (verse 8). He knew where the "red-light" area was. He went during the dark of night (verse 9). Men love darkness because their deeds are evil (John 3:19). In the bars, the less light, the more sin.

It did not take long for the foolish young man to find a woman. Her "attire of an harlot" revealed what she was (Verse 10). He is no match for her even if he wanted to be. She was subtle [crafty] of heart. He was void of understanding (Verse 7). She wasted no time pursuing her evil goal. Yet, she tried to disguise her intentions by saying she has paid her religious vows (Verse 14). She caught him kissed him, and said she had a beautiful and perfumed bed waiting. **Perfume** for centuries has been part of the bait. Note the names of some of them like *My Sin* and *Evening in Paris*.

She spoke of this sin of lust as being love and said they could "delight ourselves with love until morning" (Verse 28, NKJV). She assured him he would be safe because her husband is not home and won't be back for a long time. Be warned: If she is alone, leave her alone!

With flattery she forced him and he yielded and went after her straightway, as an ox goeth to the slaughter. His blind folly is evidenced by the statement he knoweth not that it was for his life. (Verse 23) He was only one of her   many foolish victims. Strong men had been slain by her. Samson, the strongest man that ever lived was a victim of such. So was Solomon, the wisest man, yea, even the man who penned these Words! And so was David, the man "after God's own heart." This section closes with the emphatic warning that her house is the way to hell. (Verse 27)

What God Says This Sin will Cost you

Every person who commits this sin will be hurt. You can no more commit this and not suffer than you can walk on hot coals and not be burned. *Whosoever toucheth her shall not be innocent.* (7:27-29, 32) The *Playboy* philosophy is that this is okay as long as no one gets hurt. That cannot happen. Everyone always gets hurt and even hurts others.

Everyone who commits this sin *lacketh understanding* (6:32). All sin is dumb as well as wrong. The first sin back in the Garden of Eden was completely unnecessary and so are all the others.

Consider all that
This Sin will Cost you

- Your honor (5:9)
- Your wealth (5:10)
- Your health (5:11)
- *And thou mourn at the last, when thy flesh and thy body are consumed.* This is AIDS and venereal disease. Both are epidemic today.
- Possibly your life at the hands of a jealous husband (6:34-35)
- Your reputation will be permanently damaged (6:33)
- Your sin will cause you regrets and you will hate yourself (5:12-13)
- Your soul (6:32)

Some of the above are so evident, they need no comment. Regarding the others, the warnings at the end of chapter six need more attention. Two weighty truths need to be learned and taken seriously. They reveal that adultery is no ordinary sin. Consider, first the truth that committing adultery with another man's wife can get you killed. In a jealous rage, the jealous husband will not spare. He will not think logically nor listen to anyone who tries to talk to him.

The wildest night of my life was spent trying to prevent a new Christian from killing his good friend when he learned he had been involved with his wife. I had met that friend briefly. He called me and told me what had happened and that the offended husband had called saying he was on the way over to kill him.

That made me tremble because I knew what no one else knew. I knew this threat came from a man who had the weapons, the physical strength, and knowledge on how to do what he said he was going to do. Both men were in the Navy. But the offended husband was no ordinary sailor. He was a secret CIA agent, often sent on very dangerous secret missions. I knew this because, after his recent return from such a mission during which his buddy was killed, he was grieving deeply. Sworn to secrecy, he could not talk to anyone. Believing he could trust me, and saying he just had to talk to someone, he had shared the sad story with me.

My advice to the man threatened was to leave. "Where can I go?" he asked. "I don't care," I said. "Just get out of there." He left and I headed to his apartment, arriving before a fully armed, raging jealous husband. Not bothering to knock, he burst through the door screaming, "Where is he?" I'll never forget the look in his eyes. They looked like they were on fire! I don't remember ever being more scared. Not finding the man he wanted to kill, he soon left. For hours, I searched for him, going to his house trying to calm his wife and boys. The kids were screaming and ran out onto the dark street into a pouring rain.

With things somewhat settled down, I returned home at about 4:30 a.m. I met with my friend, the jealous husband, and his wife the next morning. Both were now calm, ready to listen, and pray. God was working in their lives. There was no question about her unfaithfulness, but now her husband confessed he had violated his wedding vows in the past while he was overseas. They made it right with each other and with God. That is always a must because nothing is ever right until it is right with Him. That has now been many years ago. They are together and conscientiously living for our Lord. They raised their three boys and are grateful to God for what didn't happen that wild night.

As is so common in our area, they eventually moved away. He finished his Navy career and started a business. Although several hours away, he came to visit occasionally. On one of those visits, on a Wednesday night, I was teaching a class of about fifty adults. He was there and spoke to the class. Pointing to me he said, "That man saved my life. If it hadn't been for him, I would have done something that would have put me in prison for life or maybe worse. I would never have been able to have raised my boys or spent my life with my wife." The same would have been true for the other man also.

The second solemn truth regarding this sin is just as serious if not more so. It is in the closing verses of Proverbs 6 and deals with the fact that this sin brings a *reproach that shall not be wiped away.* (6:33) The passage explains that if a thief steals food when he is hungry, people will forgive and forget. Not so when dealing with adultery. The reputation of the guilty party is ruined for life. God can and will forgive when it is confessed and forsaken. That is what David did in Psalm 51 and wrote out his confession for the world to read. People may forgive, but they will not forget.

In the mind of this writer and many others, this sin is such that, if a minister of the gospel commits it, he is disqualified from the pulpit for life. I have checked with a number of leading pastors and teachers regarding this. Almost all agreed. However, this is swiftly changing today. It is sad that this sin, indeed all sin, is taken so lightly today. Consider the following:

"What is shocking to me is how frequently Christian leaders sin grossly, then step back into leadership almost as soon as the publicity dies away. Some time ago I received a cassette tape that disturbed me greatly. It was a recording of the re-commissioning service of a pastor who had made national news by confessing to an adulterous affair. After little more than a year of 'counseling and rehabilitation,' this man was returning to public ministry with his church's blessing.

"This is happening everywhere. Restoration teams -- quipped with manuals to instruct the church on how to reinstate their fallen pastor--wait like tow-truck drivers on the side of the highway, anticipating the next leadership 'accident.'"[12]

This is tragic, both for the preacher and the church. May none of us be numbered with the flock of *Fools that make a mock at sin.* (Proverbs 14:9)

God's Wonderful Alternative to Adultery

Nevertheless, to avoid fornication, let every man have his own wife, and let every woman have her own husband. (1 Corinthians 7:2)

God-designed Holy Matrimony: When Satan approached Eve in Eden, tempting her to eat of the fruit God had forbidden, he insinuated that God was unkind by withholding from her something that was good and beneficial. True to his nature, the "father" of lies (John 8:44) lied to Eve and slandered our Lord. Everything—absolutely everything Adam and Eve needed to live and be perfectly happy was provided to them in their perfect environment by a gracious and loving God. He has not changed. For every God-given desire He gave us, He has made provision for it to be legitimately satisfied. That includes the physical desire for intimacy with the opposite sex. He made the provision for Adam and Eve when they were still in their innocence when He made Eve for Adam, brought her to him, and joined them in marriage. Of that relationship within the bond of holy matrimony, the writer of Hebrews said *Marriage is honourable in all, and the bed undefiled: but whoremongers and adulterers God will judge.* (13:4)

It is interesting and refreshing that in this key passage that deals with the blight of adultery, God injected the bliss of marital love (Proverbs 5:15-20). In discreet, but unmistakable terms, God describes the intimate physical relationship of a man and wife. He says he is to *rejoice with the wife of his youth* and be *ravished always with her love* (verses 18-19). Then he asked, in light of this, *Why wilt thou, my son, be ravished with a strange woman* (verse 20), especially since *the ways of man are before the eyes of the Lord* .(verse 21 God sees all this and will see to it that *His own iniquities shall take the wicked himself, and he shall be holden* [enslaved] *with the cords of his sins. He shall die without instruction; and in the greatness of his folly he shall go astray.* (Verses 22: 23)

What a terrible thing it is to swap this beautiful and holy marriage love that God created and that pictures something of our loving relationship with Jesus Christ (He is the Bridegroom, the church is His bride) for a vile, selfish, and lustful relationship that carries such awful consequences!

This sin is wrong for so many reasons, not least of which is how it destroys that God-designed picture of the relationship between His Son and His church. Find that recorded in Ephesians chapter five. That passage is where we read *For this cause shall a man leave his father and mother* [a great love relationship], *and shall be joined unto his wife* [a greater love] *and they two shall be one flesh. This is a great mystery: but I speak concerning Christ and the Church. Nevertheless let every one of you in particular so love his wife even as himself; and the wife see that she reverence her husband.* (Ephesians 5:31-33) That, beloved, is our loving God's answer to the sin of adultery. Be sure you choose and teach your children to choose the better part.

God's Inspired Word: *Thy word have I hid in mine heart, that I might not sin against thee.* (Psalm 119:11) There may be no more important time where this truth is needed than when we are tempted by the sin of adultery. God knew that and, in those three chapters in Proverbs (5-7), had Solomon often urge his son to heed his words, his mother's, and God's. Confronted face to face with temptation coming directly from the devil, in all three situations, Jesus rebutted him with the words, "It is written..." (Matthew 3:1-10) The apostle John wrote, *I have written unto you, fathers, because ye have known him that is from the beginning. I have written unto you, young men, because ye are strong, and the word of God abideth in you, and ye have* *overcome the wicked one.* (1 John 2:14)

Notice he says to the "young men, ye are strong." If anyone needs God's strength in this area, it is our youth. Notice also, the source of their strength was "the word of God" that abided in them. This was the key to their being able to "overcome the wicked one." The prophet Hosea explained why so many of even God's people fall prey to sin: *My people are destroyed for lack of knowledge.* (Hosea 4:6) The absence and ignorance of the God's Word today has contributed to the corruption of our youth as nothing else. Neither the pulpits, the parents, nor our places of worship are innocent regarding this famine of the Word of God.

Psalm 119:11

Thy Word – The Best Thing
Hidden in my Heart — In The Best Place
That I Might Not Sin Against God — For the Best Purpose
-- Charles Spurgeon

A Bouquet to God's Most Beautiful Creation

Have you ever thought about how God's final act of creation was His most beautiful? That, of course, was when He made woman. In the animal kingdom, the male is usually the more attractive while the female is often plain and not as quick to catch your eye. When it comes to human beings, most normal men would agree the order is reversed. When God created woman, He endowed her with a lot of natural beauty. She really does not require a lot of man-made additions from high-dollar "paint and body shops" to make her beautiful. It is amazing how godly ladies dressed in simple, feminine fashion can be very attractive even into their senior years.

It is interesting how Peter, in instructing ladies how to win their unsaved husbands, while first telling them their lives must be pure and reverent, then spoke of how they are to be adorned in order to enhance their testimony.

Whose adorning let it not be that outward adorning of plaiting the hair, and of wearing of gold, or of putting on of apparel; But let it be the hidden man of the heart, in that which is not corruptible, even the ornament of a meek and quiet spirit, which is in the sight of God of great price. (1 Peter 3:3-5)

This passage is sometimes taken to mean ladies should not wear any jewelry. If it means no jewelry, then it means no clothes (apparel). Of course, it certainly does not mean that. Instead, Peter is telling them the flashy things of the world are useless in trying to win their unsaved mates. Being modestly adorned like godly women have always dressed, coupled with a "meek and quiet spirit" will help in situations even when she is not free to use God's word (verse 1). Add to that the words of the wise man from the chapter on the virtuous woman: *Favor is deceitful and beauty is vain: but a woman that feareth the LORD, she shall be praised.* (Proverbs 31:30)

Along with the bouquet above, ladies allow me to do a little teaching, or preaching if you insist. May I remind you there are myriads of available women out there who are looking for a man. The bars are filled nightly with a scantily clad crowd counting on the bait of bearing their bodies to catch a man. And they may. A man just like themselves. A selfish soul seeking someone to make him happy just as she is looking for someone to make her happy. So two selfish souls link up briefly and make each other unhappy. Such relationships are based on lust, the opposite of love. Lust says "I want you to make me happy." Love says "I want you so I can make you happy."

Ladies, please listen to the God who loves you. Learn this and teach it to your daughters. God made you and, in almost every case, plans for you to have a good husband. But if you will not follow His holy instructions, and instead insist on getting your man with your body, be warned. There are many out there with bodies more beautiful than yours (especially as you get older) who are willing to do whatever it takes to lure him away from you. Play that game and you will join multitudes who have paid the price and who will go home alone again tonight to a tiny apartment and a tiny baby.

Chapter Ten

Honoring The Lord's Day

I was in the Spirit on the Lord's day. (Revelation 1:10)

At the time of this writing, we are only a few days removed from celebrating Christmas. As typical in recent years, we have been saddened to see this Special Day in the Christian's calendar so abused. Many of us, as we do each year, complained at being greeted with "Happy Holidays" instead of honoring Jesus' birth by saying "Merry Christmas." As believers, we want to put Christ back into Christmas, but while there is nothing wrong with setting aside a special day to honor our Savior's birth, there is nothing in the Bible instructing us to do so. It is great we have done that for centuries, reminding the world every year that a Savior has come and that His name is Jesus.

However, consider for a moment the abuse of fifty-two other special days in the year that are taught in God's Word—The Lord's Day! As we have grieved over how the unsaved world has so desecrated Christmas, making it a holiday for their own selfish enjoyment, we need to take a serious look at what the Lord's own people are doing to His Day. Our study may cause us to recall the proverb from Luke 4:23 *Physician heal thyself.*

Any study of this special day must begin with its predecessor, where we read in Geneses 2:3 *God blessed the seventh day, and sanctified it: because that in it he had rested from all his work which God created and made.* (Genesis 2:3)

From the beginning of the world, one day out of seven was

fenced off by God as His own peculiar property. It was to be a "holy" (separate, "sanctified") day (Exodus 20:8). From its inception, it had a two-fold purpose. In reference to God, it was to be a time when man, the epitome of God's creation, made in His likeness and image, would pause to honor and worship his Creator.

Regarding man, it was to be a time of rest from his labors, which Adam had in Eden (Genesis 2:15), even before his fall into sin. Rest presupposes labor. Man was to labor six days (Exodus 20:9) and would therefore need a day of rest. That explains why Jesus said *The sabbath was made for man, and not man for the Sabbath.* (Mark 2:27) Whatever these two things involve, as we shall show, it is clear that they both are applicable to all mankind in every age and not only to the Jews in the Old Testament.

Regarding the word "Sabbath" (it means rest, or decease) most of you reading this will be aware that the Old Testament Sabbath was on Saturday, the seventh day of the week, and that the Lord's Day is Sunday, the first day of the week. That change occurred after Jesus was resurrected and in honor of His resurrection. We know that took place on Sunday. From that time forward, as recorded in the New Testament (Matthew 28:1 and all the gospels, Acts 20:7, 1 Corinthians 16:2), Christians honored Jesus on that day as their main day of worship. Hence, it became known as "the Lord's Day." (Revelation 1:10)

Before discussing how we should properly observe the Lord's Day, we need to consider how the idea of one day in seven was set aside as a special day for God's people and how it was carried through all the Old Testament. We need to see how, though the day has changed, the need for such a day and the principle involved in it have not. In seeing that, we will see it is incumbent on all people to cease their own pursuits and pause and worship our Creator. That being so, it follows there must be a time in which that is to be done. History has proven that God has guided in that day being changed from Saturday to Sunday. His day—the Lord's Day that must be honored.

The first of the Ten Commandments instructs us we are to worship God and only Him. The fourth dictates a day for that to be done. Sunday has appropriately been that day since Jesus' resurrection. If Sunday is crowded out, is Monday or any other day going to be crowned His Day?

Pastor A.B. Brown, my associate for about ten years, has written a timely booklet on this subject in which he says, "There are two basic questions the Christian must ask with regard to the Lord's Day. First, he must ask if the Church was correct in transferring its day of worship from the Sabbath (the seventh day of the week) to the Lord's Day (the first day of the week)? If, as he concludes that the Church was justified in doing so, he must ask if there are any Biblical guidelines regarding our observation of this day?" He added, "The purpose of his study is to set forth the proposition that the answer to both of these questions is in the affirmative."

From the Sabbath to Sunday, The Lord's Day

Adam and Eve brought two special institutions out of Eden with them: Marriage and the Sabbath. Both were ordained by God and given to Adam even prior to their fall into sin. Both have been severely attacked and maligned today. Human reasoning has said marriage just evolved over time and is no longer needed. Some naive students of scripture think the Sabbath was instituted by Moses and was only for the Jews. They are wrong on both counts. Tracing the history of the Sabbath in the Old Testament you will find that the Sabbath

- **Was instituted in Eden for man and to honor God. (Genesis 2:3)**

- Was revived in the wilderness. When God gave the Jews manna from heaven, He instructed them that they were to gather it for six days, "but not on the Sabbath." (Exodus 16:26) That was before the Ten Commandments were given.

- Was given by God through Moses as a direct commandment. *Remember the Sabbath Day to keep it holy.* (Exodus 20:8) Please notice the word "Remember." It occurs only in reference to this commandment and proves it had been in existence for centuries.

- Was confirmed by the practice of our Lord and the apostles. *He came to Nazareth, where he had been brought up: and, as his custom was, he went into the synagogue on the sabbath day, and stood up for to read.* (Luke 4:16)

Noting the commandment "Remember the Sabbath, to keep it holy" comes between those that speak of our duty to God and then to man, some have seen in violating this commandment a direct insult to God and is a direct injury to man. To be sure, this command from our loving Lord is a blessing to the human race and we are the loosers when we disobey it.

Does anyone want to argue that adultery or murder was not wrong prior to the giving of the Ten Commandments? The same rational should be applied to those who say the commandment regarding the Sabbath does not apply to believers today. If it does not, neither do the other nine. Jesus said *Think not that I am come to destroy the law, or the prophets: I am not come to destroy, but to fulfill.* (Matthew 5:17) He fulfilled the ceremonial law. We are not obligated to keep it. Not so with the moral law. It, like our moral Creator, does not change. The day has changed, but not the principles. Our bodies need rest and we need to have a regular, specified time to worship our Lord and meet with His people today just like the Jews did in the Old Testament.

Add to these reasons, the Sabbath was a time when the Jews celebrated their redemption from Egyptian slavery. *And remember that thou wast a servant in the land of Egypt, and that the Lord thy God brought thee out thence through a mighty hand and by a stretched out arm: therefore the Lord thy God commanded thee to keep the sabbath day.* (Deuteronomy 5:15)

If they needed to regularly remember being redeemed from the rigors of Egyptian bondage, how much more should we often and regularly assemble with His redeemed Church, praising Him for saving us from the bondage and misery of our sins and the unending fires of hell? The Sabbath not only gave God's redeemed people reason to meet and praise God for their redemption from sin's' penalty, it also pointed to a place of rest far superior to the earthly Canaan. General Joshua led Israel into a temporary rest in Canaan, but our Joshua (the name is Jesus in Greek) will soon take us into the eternal resting place called heaven. *There remaineth therefore a rest to the people of God.* (Hebrews 4:9)

An Objection

Romans 14:5-6: *One man esteemeth one day above another: another esteemeth every day alike. Let every man be fully persuaded in his own mind.*

In the Biblical Illustrator, the Cadillac of commentaries for sermon building, R. Wardlaw, states in these verses Paul had reference to the "observances distinctly Jewish" and not the day God "instituted for mankind at the creation." He said the question was about days of Jewish observance and no one would think of this referring to Sunday. He argued that to say that if that had been included, "it would follow that here was a church that had no fixed observance of social worship, but every one left to do what was 'right in his own eyes.'" He added, "Whether such a state of things will be consistent with that God who is not the Author of confusion, I leave you to judge. The passage, therefore, having reference to Jewish days of the week, does not in the least invalidate the fact of the observance of the first day, as if it had no place in the days of dispute."[13]

More could be said regarding the change from the Old Testament Sabbath to the Lord's Day in the New Testament, but, with one more bit of evidence, we believe the point will have been made. Consider what scripture records regarding the ministry of the apostle Paul during the early days of the Church. References to the churches in Philippi (Acts 20:7) and Corinth (1 Corinthians 16:1, 2) meeting on the Lord's Day proves this was no isolated practice.

In Acts 15 a great number of churches came together to confront and decide the issue of the Gentiles being saved, but not being required to be circumcised and taught to keep the Old Testament Law. They decided that Paul's message of grace to the Gentiles was right. Circumcision was not essential. The point here is this: That if those saying the Old Testament Law had to be kept to be right with God, surely the issue regarding the Sabbath would have been mentioned. It was not. Why? Because the Church had now made the transition to the Lord's Day as evidenced by the Scriptures. The testimony of such early Church Fathers as Ignatius, Barnabas, and Justin Martyr confirmed this.

From the time of Jesus' resurrection until the present,

there is an unbroken history of Sunday as the special day Christians have observed as the day we are to meet and worship. It was indeed the literal, bodily resurrection of our Savior from the dead that led to this change from the Sabbath of the Old Testament. It certainly was not brought about much later by the Roman Catholic Church, nor was it done by heathen, in honor of worshipping the sun (Sun- Sunday) as some cults like the Seventh Day Adventist claim. All the days of the week are named after heavenly bodies. Monday for the moon, etc.

"Paradise, with its calm, its purity, and its beauty is gone; but the Sabbath with Paradise is not. It has accompanied man in sorrows, as it accompanied him in his joy."
-H. Stowell [14]

Laws for the Lord's Day: Boundaries But Not Bondage

Two things we need to keep in mind from the previous section are (1) we have shown that the Sabbath of the Old Testament began in Eden prior to Adam and Eve's sin and did not originate at the time God delivered Moses the Ten Commandments hundreds of years later. It was therefore applicable to all people from the beginning and not only the Jews. (2) Secondly, that the transfer of the Old Testament Sabbath to the Lord's Day in the New Testament was clearly the practice of the New Testament church and has been throughout history. The inspired biblical record that reveals this change is testimony to the fact God approved the transition.

The *day* has been changed, but not the moral principles. They cannot because our holy God cannot change (Hebrews 13:8). Now we are confronted with the question, How are we to observe the Lord's Day? Are there guiding principles given to us in scripture or are we all left to figure it out on our own? If there are moral principles involved, and there are, we are not left to our own judgment to decide what is right and what is wrong. Only our righteous Creator has the right to decide that. *O Lord, I know that the way of man is not in himself: it is not in man that walketh to direct his steps.* (Jeremiah 10:23)

A Day of Rest: As we ponder this question, some things are apparent. Our gracious and loving God, who, out of His concern for our physical, social, and spiritual well-being, ordained the original day of rest, has not changed and therefore has ordained the same for the Lord's Day. It does not follow, however, that we are under obligation to follow every detail on the Lord's Day that the Jews were to follow as given by Moses. Those were a sign of the covenant God made between himself and Israel. (Exodus 31:13, 17) They would not work for the entire world. For example, the Jewish Sabbath was from sundown on Friday until sundown on Saturday. The sun doesn't go down every day at the north or south poles. That does not alter the fact that the *principles* of one day remain the same.

Before we proceed to list the proper ways to observe the Lord's Day, let us say to the church, we are not to copy the example of the Pharisees in the New Testament who added myriads of ridiculous man-made regulations as to how the Sabbath was to be observed. Jesus had some harsh words for them. This legalistic approach destroys what God had in mind when He instituted this special day of rest and worship. An early and eloquent preacher in the colonial days of America aptly said,

> "A week filled with selfishness and a Sabbath filled full of religious exercises, will make a good Pharisee, but a poor Christian."
>
> --(H. W. Beecher)[15]

A Day of Worship: This too is clearly one of the things God intended to mark His Day. This was true of the church in the book of Acts. (20:7) That was not just true of private worship, but meant believers were to meet together to learn the Word of God and help encourage and support one another. God has given His church leaders such as *evangelists; and some, pastors and teachers;* [to enable us to] *grow in grace, and in the knowledge of our Lord and Saviour Jesus Christ. To him be glory both now and forever. Amen.* (2 Peter 3:18)

How are we going to learn from God's messengers and grow in God's grace if we are absent when the truth we need is given. A vital part of what the early Christians did on the Lord's day was meet with fellow believers, learn the Word of God, pray together, and get prepared to go out and share the gospel with others. All of that and more is what is involved in the main verse in the Bible that tells the Christian to faithfully attend church: *Not forsaking the assembling of ourselves together, as the manner of some is; but exhorting one another: and so much the more, as ye see the day approaching.* (Hebrews 10:25)

Please note the word "assembling." Christian workers will tell you they often have professing Christians tell them they either have church at home with their family or watch a church service on TV. That "electronic" church service is like watching those cooking shows on TV. You won't get nourished by just watching! And who is your pastor? Who will you call on when you need a man of God? And where are you going to take your lost family and friends where you know they will hear the real gospel and a real person will follow up with them? Where do you send your tithe and what world missions program are you involved in? The work of God would have died long ago if all professing Christians were like that. If you are such a professor, you may need to check up and see if you are really one of Jesus' sheep. If you are, your disobedience shows you are away from Him and any sheep away from the Shepherd is an easy prey for the devil, that roaring lion that is seeking whom he may devour. (1 Peter 5:8).

When God inspired the writing of Hebrews 10:25, He knew there would be TV and videos in the future. Still, He said we are to assemble together. The verse tells us why--to exhort and encourage one another. After battling the world all week, what a blessing it is to gather where we can get a breath of pure air! We need this at all times, but especially in times like today when we are much in the minority and headed into persecution. That was the situation the Jewish believers were facing. Yet, even in the face of grave danger, they were still instructed to assemble with God's people. Persecution is swiftly coming upon believers today. The following verses in Hebrews 10 paint a scary future ahead for those who do not heed this command from the Lord.

The application of the above two principles is clear. Activities on the Lord's Day that prevent us from meeting with God's people for worship are wrong. That does not include such things as "providential" situations. We will discuss those soon. But it does apply to things you choose for selfish pleasure or profit. Things like sports or working on the Lord's Day to get time and a half. (Soon, more from Matthew 12 on the exceptions to working on the Lord's Day.) Think on the masses every Lord's Day that miss church, spend many hours and big bucks filling the gigantic ball stadiums, NASCAR race tracks, arenas, beaches, crowding the golf courses, lakes and rivers. A large percentage of them profess to be saved. They are desecrating the Lord's Day. That is sin. A little prayer said over the P.A. System before the game or before they start their engines doesn't change that. In fact, to the degree it stifles conviction, it makes things worse.

Two more warnings need to be sounded. Worship on the Lord's Day involves meeting with God's people, in as much as is possible (and it usually is) in the "house of the Lord" (Psalm 122:1). Sitting somewhere on Sunday mornings and watching the sun rise does not count. Regarding the Lord's Day as a day of rest, that rules out dropping in a church service for an hour and then going on to work or even (I've seen this many times) bringing your business materials with you, lugging it home with you, and ending up back at work the next day to drop down at your desk more exhausted than you were when you left on Friday. The same passage that says one Day belongs to God, says *Six days thou shalt labor and do all thy work.* (Exodus 20:9) If you have too much to do to get it done in six days, you have more to do than God wants you to try to do. It has been proven many times that man and beast can do more in six days than they can in seven. Like the Sabbath, the Lord's Day was made for you. Use it like God intended and you will be blessed.

Those who talk to others about this matter hear often, "I don't believe you have to go to church to be a Christian." That reveals a couple of things: First, they don't want to go to church, which tells us they don't share believers' hearts. (1 John 3:14) We *know that we have passed from death unto life, because we love the brethren.* (1 John 3:14)

Secondly, they don't understand what God has said on this subject. A married man doesn't have to go home to be married, but it sure works a lot better if he does. If he doesn't, there are serious problems. There is another side to this also. If you are indeed born again, and willfully missing church, Hebrews 12 has some solemn words for you. God is a good Father, and is serious about His children. If they will not obey, because He loves them, He promises He will "chastise every son whom he receiveth," and adds, that such a spiritual spanking will not be "joyous." (12:6, 11)

The New Testament knows nothing of Christians who willfully did not assemble with the Lord's Church. When Paul, (previously called Saul), was saved, he immediately tried to join other believers. *When Saul was come to Jerusalem, he assayed* [tried] *to join himself to the disciples: but they were all afraid of him, and believed not that he was a disciple.* (Acts 9:26) Barnabas went to him, checked him out, and vouched for his conversion.

A Holy Day: The word means set apart. Regarding the Lord's Day, it means we should, as best we can, come apart from the secular and routine of life and make it a special day of fellowship with our Lord and His people, yes, and our families. Reading a little extra in God's Word, stealing away for some extra time in prayer, reading a good devotional book or missionary biography is great. A visit to a shut-in brother or sister can be a blessing to you and them. Remember holiness and happiness go together. Read the beatitudes again. The word "Blessed" there is in the plural. They are multiplied.

The Lord's Day—A Delight

Satan is a master deceiver. His greatest trap is luring us with his lies. He told Eve, she would not die for disobeying God, but rather she would find pleasure. Talk to unsaved hearts about the proper use of the Lord's Day and they think we are the ones who are deceived. Indeed, like John Newton, the sordid sailor, who, after his conversion, wrote the great hymn *Amazing Grace*, and told the truth with the words, *I once was blind but now I see.* The apostle Paul agreed. Scales fell from his eyes when he gave his life to Christ. (Acts 9:18) He wrote later *the god of this world* [Satan] *hath blinded the minds of them which believe not, lest the light of the glorious gospel of Christ, who is the image of God, should shine unto them.* (2 Corinthians 4:4) How sad and dangerous it is to be blind and not know you are blind.

Regarding the misconception that says living for Jesus and going to His house faithfully to worship Him will make you miserable, listen to the great prophet, Isaiah:

If thou turn away thy foot from the sabbath, from doing thy pleasure on my holy day; and call the sabbath a delight, the holy of the Lord, honourable; and shalt honour him, not doing thine own ways, nor finding thine own pleasure, nor speaking thine own words: Lord; and I will cause thee to ride upon the high places of the earth, and feed thee with the heritage of Jacob thy father: for the mouth of the Lord hath spoken it. (Isaiah 58:13-14)

The Lord's Day was very special to the Puritans. They spoke of it as the *Queen of Days,* the *golden spot of the week,* a day for entering *the very suburbs of heaven*. They warned against letting it become routine. Richard Baxter wrote how the heart must be prepared in advance, stating "the battle for our Sundays is usually won or lost on the foregoing Saturday night, when time should be set aside for self-examination, confession, and prayer for the coming day." Another added, "If thou wouldst thus leave thy heart with God on Saturday night, thou shouldst find it with him in the Lord's Day morning." It should be noted also that they met twice a day on the Lord's Day—a morning and evening service. They considered the Lord's day was all day, not just an hour on Sunday morning, or in some cases today, on Saturday night.

Baxter had a practical rule worth heeding: "Go seasonably to bed that you may not be sleepy on the Lord's Day." Still on the practical side, he said we should get up early on the Lord's Day, have our devotions, and not become rushed and fussy getting to church, noting, if we do "The Word shall be but tediousness and serve to the further hardening of the heart." He had a word for the preachers also: "Preach with such life and awakening seriousness...that the people will never be weary of you."

This was not the advice of a professor in some cloistered classroom, detached from the real world. Instead, it was a godly pastor who lived in God's Word and with his people. In his town of Kidderminster with a population of about 2000 adults, his habit was to rise by 3:00 each morning and be in the streets five mornings a week to pray and preach to people before they went to the fields. He usually had a considerable congregation. He opened his home two days a week to families, usually interviewing and disciplining seven or eight each day. They often left in tears.

As a visible testimony to this abundance of spiritual fruit, his church building when he went there that seated about a thousand, had added five galleries by the time he left nineteen years later. He described the town when he went as "an ignorant, rude, and reveling people, who for the most part...had hardly ever had lively, serious preaching.-" When he left, "On the Lord's Day, there was no disorder to be seen in the Streets, but you might hear an hundred families singing Psalms and repeating Sermons, as you passed through the streets."

Read these stories and feel sorry for those who mistakenly call these godly people ignorant and, hoping to demean them, contemptuously label them "puritanical." More, feel ashamed for those of us who are Christians, but who know so little about such genuine godliness. You can be assured that these humble, holy people would not have lived and labored as they did year after year if they were not finding genuine joy in serving Jesus. Like David, they were glad (not sad) *when they said unto me, Let us go into the house of the Lord.* (Psalm 122:1)

Rightly Remembering the Sabbath
(Our Lord's Day) To Keep it Holy

To most today, Sunday is "Run Day" or "Fun Day" or if you live near the beach it is "Sun Day." In contrast, we believe we have established the fact that the New Testament Lord's Day is to be a special day for believers. We have noted this day is to be a day of rest, worship of our God, and it is to be observed as a "holy" day, meaning it is to be devoted to God and we are to be, as much as possible, separated from the usual pursuits of life. We are now going to look at specific activities and ask whether or not they violate these purposes God has given us. Before we beg in, we need to again be reminded not to follow the Pharisees whom Jesus seriously rebuked for destroying the very purpose of the Sabbath with the mountain of man-made traditions they added to what God had said. (Mark 7:5-9) What God designed to be a blessing to us, became a burden.

Working on Sunday: Accepting the position that the Lord's Day is to be a day of rest, and worship set apart for God, the first question to ask is, What about working on Sunday? We have earlier referenced Exodus 20:11 where God reminded us He rested on the seventh day and hallowed and blessed it. Clearly, the principle given there that work on the Lord's Day, as we ordinarily think of it and practice it, is sin. In Matthew 12, Jesus gave four exceptions to this.

Works of Necessity: Jesus' disciples pulled some grain, rolled it in their hands, and ate it on the Sabbath. The Pharisees accused them of violating the Sabbath. Jesus defended His followers. (Matthew 12:1-4) We must eat. That requires work. They did only the basics. They did not cause others to have to work. They only violated one of the man-made traditions, not God's Word.

Two other considerations: (1) The manna from heaven that God gave the Israelites in the wilderness was doubled on the day before the Sabbath so they would not have to work gathering it on the Sabbath. (Exodus 16:5) It is wise, and very possible today, to make most of our provisions of food for the Lord's Day in advance. (2) Instructions about the Sabbath in the Old Testament were that, not only were they not to labor on the Sabbath, but they were not to involve their family or their servants in labor. Apply that to shopping or eating out on the Lord's Day. How many people working in restaurants and retail stores might be in church on the Lord's Day if Christians would not patronize their places of business on the Lord's Day?

When I attended Bible College back in the '50's, we were served a noon meal in the cafeteria and given a sack lunch for the evening meal. We would be given demerits if we were caught shopping on Sunday. A few years later, pastoring a church in that same city with several of the faculty and many of the students from the college in our services, I preached that back to those who had taught me.

During the great revival years of the past, the Lord's Day came to be greatly honored. The great evangelist, D.L. Moody would not buy a newspaper or ride the street cars on Sunday. His godly influence was such in Chicago that, not only were the stores not opened on Sunday, they draped the store windows on Saturday evening to prevent people from window shopping on the Lord's Day. My Dad did that at his General Store when I was young before we moved to the farm. I recall a couple of times when he went to the store and got food for some needy cases. Needless to say, church attendance was much better in those days. The best Bible professor I had in graduate school told us, if a community has a real revival, you will see two proofs—liquor joints closing and a renewed reverence for the Lord's Day.

Religious Work: Jesus said the priests worked on the Sabbath and were "blameless." (Matthew 12:5) Every real pastor knows Sunday is not a day of rest for him. He is at church early, preaches twice that day, and often teaches Sunday School and even a class on Sunday night before the regular service. He needs to take off a different day during the week.

Works of Mercy: On several occasions, the Pharisees accused Jesus of violating the Sabbath because he healed on the Sabbath. (12:9-12) It is apparent that hospitals cannot close on Sunday.

Works of Emergency: In the passage referenced above, Jesus pointed out the hypocrisy of the Pharisees by reminding them if one of their sheep fell in a ditch on the Sabbath, they would work to get it out on that day. Then he exposed them by saying *How much then is a man better than a sheep? Wherefore it is lawful to do well on the sabbath days.* (12:12)

The gospel of Luke speaks of an ox falling into the ditch. That is the usual way this is mentioned. Most pastors have heard lame excuses for missing church like, "Well, the ox got in the ditch." A long time ago, some got tired of hearing that and responded, "If the ox keeps getting in the ditch, you need to either fill up the ditch or kill the ox."

The major problem that keeps people working on the Lord's Day is greed. Greedy merchants and greedy employees. The employees are happy to work Sundays, often making time and a half or double time. The greedy merchants, eager to get an advantage over competitors, began opening when others were closed. Soon the others felt they too had to open to meet the competition. At first, many businesses waited until Sunday morning services were over. That didn't last long. Gradually, the "blue laws," laws restricting businesses from being open on Sunday (common in Colonial days) were declared "unconstitutional." Three judges in our area (Hampton Roads, VA) made that decision, even though twice the majority in all six municipalities voted to keep the blue laws.

In my opinion, the reason we lost to the judges is because the motive for trying to retain the blue laws was wrong. I was much involved with the Retail Merchants' Association, (the only preacher) the main entity that worked to keep the stores closed. Their approach was we need to do this to give our employees a day of rest. Honorable as that may be, that is not the main motive for Christians. We need a day of rest, but also a day to worship and honor our Savior. Before you sign up for Sunday work, remember, how you treat the Lord's Day is an indication of how you treat the Lord.

Observations: Obviously, each believer will have to pray, seek God's will about his situation, and, while being careful to follow God's Word, also consult his own conscience. If his work is clearly secular, and does not fall into one of four exceptions above, he needs to avoid it. Even if the business stays open on Sunday, it has been established in the courts that an employee can request and get time off to attend his religious services. In college, I worked two years at a place that closed only one day a year—Christmas. When I was hired, I told the boss I could not work on Sunday. He never asked me to. He checked periodically on who was doing the bulk of the work. My record was good. That helped.

As a rule, Christians should seek to get in professions where they will not ordinarily be expected to work on Sunday. Churches are desperate for workers. Unless the Lord specifically directs you otherwise, I encourage you to let others fill those secular Sunday positions so you can be faithful in God's service on His day.

One last observation: Taking a second job that involves working Sundays or jumping at opportunities to work on Sunday because you get extra pay for it should not be considered. Greed should not trump God. Many feel you cannot do this in today's world. Chick Filet and Hobby Lobby seem to be doing pretty good. Many great companies have in the past.

Christian, God has given His church *evangelists; and some, pastors and teachers; For the perfection of the saints for the work of the ministry, for the edifying of the body of Christ.* (Ephesians 4:11-12). They are there for you and your family. Be there to hear them.

Enjoyable Things to Do on the Lord's Day

Before getting into the specifics where there will of necessity be some negatives, take a few minutes to think of some of the things believers can and should do on the Lord's Day. How about making a visit to a lonely shut-in, encouraging them and praying with them? Taking some of your family with you can also be a blessing. If the weather is pretty, how about a drive in the country. Seeing God's great creation, away from the noise of the city, can be an inspiring experience. Any day, but especially on days you are shut in because of the weather, reading a good book, maybe a biography of some great missionary like Adoniram Judson or Hudson Taylor or the bestselling book of all time outside the Bible, *Pilgrim's Progress* by John Bunyan. The story of these men's lives will touch your heart and challenge you for Christ.

You don't have to be a bookworm to enjoy such reading. I was not. I never took a book home in High School. I became an avid reader only after getting serious about serving the Lord. Good, godly, music in the background can sometimes make your reading even more a joy. There are so many more beneficial and enjoyable things you can do on the Lord's Day. A nap on Sunday afternoon is especially nice for many who can't get one on other days. It refreshes you for the evening service at church also. Talk to good Christians to learn more. As a button on my desk that I had made up and distributed when we were in a battle to keep the stores closed on Sundays says "Don't Let Them Sell out Our Sundays." And don't let the devil or your flesh lure you into doing it. We don't like to face it, but the TV and the internet are the Big Thieves of our Lord's Days. Once again, remember, the way you treat the Lord's Day is the way you treat the Lord.

More Questions on Specific Activities

In his letter to the Galatians, Paul told believers who were being bewitched by false teachers, that since Calvary and, since the Holy Spirit has come into our hearts, we are no longer like little children, but are treated as adult sons. (Chapters 3 and 4) As such, we should be able to live and act according to the principles God has given us rather than to have to be told what to do or what not to do with regard to every issue. This writer believes that this policy comes into play in deciding what you can do and/or should not do to keep the Lord's Day holy. The New Testament does not spell out what is proper in every situation, but in keeping with the principles we know, if we sincerely desire to honor our Savior and His Day, the Holy Spirit will guide us in making the right decisions.

Reviewing, what we know is that the Lord's Day is to be fenced in as a day of rest, worship, and is to be a "holy" day, separated from the secular and unto God. We know too, that it was made for man and not man for the Sabbath. Man is a physical, spiritual, and social creature. These things are also of legitimate concern in making these decisions.

In the physical area, we need a time for rest, but not a day of idleness. In the spiritual area, as believers, we certainly need and have reason to truly worship our Savior. As a social creature, we need social interaction with others, especially our families and our spiritual brothers and sisters. Surely, there are activities that are acceptable in all of these areas. Keep in mind too, that the entire day is the "holy" Lord's Day and we must be discerning lest we fall for some of the devil's diversions and slide back into the secular. That danger is very real. Consider some specifics:

Sports: Signing up to play with a team whose games and/or practices will keep you from being faithful in church causes a lot of Christians to miss church. "Well, I promised I would be faithful to the team," they may say. What about the promise you made to be faithful to Jesus?

Our world has gone crazy over sports. Even many of us who never excelled in any of them like to watch the games. Most want their children to be involved in them. Many seem to try to relive their lives through their children. They love it when they excel. Someone said, many parents would rather their children be stars than saints. Sports per se are not wrong unless you put them first. That's true of many things. Many become sports addicts. It dominates their lives, takes a large part of their time and money, and is their main topic of conversation. Cozy up to a group of preachers at a break at one of their meetings, especially if it's a Monday morning, and most likely what you will hear is a rehashing of the NFL or NBA from Sunday's games.

God's children have no business being involved in professional sports or any events sponsored by the world on the Lord's Day. The very atmosphere will hinder you from being what God intended the day to be and time involved in them is probably going to prevent you from being faithful in church, from being faithful in having your devotions, and even getting the rest you need. Many get so involved in such activities, they get up early, drive for miles, exert so much energy, and spend so much money, when they show up for work on Monday they are bushed and broke. There is also the matter of time that could have been spent with your family that has been ill-spent.

Harkening back to the professional sporting events, your presence and your money are perpetuating keeping those participating in these events out of church. Questions you need to consider are ones like, since everything we do should be done to the glory of God (1 Corinthians 10:31), we must ask, "Can I do this to His glory on His Day?" "Would Jesus go with me to this event on Sunday?" "Or even sit and watch it on TV with me?"

Church Activities That are not Church

Now in this that I declare unto you I praise you not, that ye

come together not for the better, but for the worse.
(1 Corinthians 11:17)

Yes, it is possible to be worse for going to some so-called church services/and or activities. That was the case with the carnal Corinthian Church. There were divisions, gluttony, drunkenness, and the Lord's Supper was a mockery. Hopefully, no one reading these pages is involved in anything like that. But consider some things that might be more familiar.

How about Sunday night services being taken over by the sports craze like Super Bowl Sunday? It started back in the '60's. A TV (the bigger the better) was brought in. Popcorn and soft drinks were supplied. The congregation fellowshipped as they watched the game.

Sometime during the evening (This service lasted about three times as long as the usual Sunday night service.) there was usually a brief devotion. It was apparent that was only to calm their consciences and not the main reason most had come. At first, the more consecrated complained. Ignored, they sometimes moved their membership, or just became silent and skipped such "services." A deacon from a church in Tennessee called me about such a service in his church. He said when he came in for church on Sunday morning there were twenty-one footballs hanging from the ceiling of the church. He, along with a handful of others, soon left.

Sad to say, such desecration of the Lord's Day and the Lord's house is not confined to only one day in the year. Warm weather provides more opportunities to bring in more sports and purely social events. Badminton, soft ball or baseball, horse shoes—you name it, you can find it all on the church yard or a nearby ball field on Sunday nights, all sponsored by a church. There, while, there may be a prayer, the devotion is usually dropped.

God's servants, with hearts for holiness and a desire to win lost souls, grieve over these things. A missionary couple (now deceased) who were friends of mine attended such a service while they were home on furlough at a church where their son was on the staff. A platform for the band had been erected on the church lawn and would remain there for the duration of the summer. The people gathered, dressed for the non-church activity, and joined in the games while listening to today's contemporary music. The wife of this experienced missionary soon turned to him and said, "Take me home. This is not church and I don't want to stay here." If such has not yet arrived at your church, be warned. It is likely on the way.

Closing Comments on The Lord's Day

In the New Testament era, even though most of the believers were some sort of slaves (90% of the Roman Empire was), they found a way to meet with Christ's Church on His Day. How different from our day where the desire for profit and pleasure keeps the majority of professing Christians from church on any given Sunday. The sports stadiums are full. The golf courses crowded, the lakes and beaches densely populated, and most businesses are open. About the only thing you can't find open is a church on Sunday night. Wonder how much of this is the fault of the preachers today? Listen to them talk when they get together. Sports, not the Savior, will usually be the main topic. Many spent so much time on Sunday afternoon watching their favorite team until they were neither prepared or in the mood to conduct a church service that evening.

Any church, community, or nation that disregards and dishonors the Lord's Day will sink deeper into sin and suffer the consequences. History shows God has blessed His Day and those who honor it. The opposite is also true. A graphic example of that is the Jewish nation. In 586 B.C. the barbaric Babylonians conquered that privileged people, leveling the capital city of Jerusalem including the magnificent King Solomon's Temple. They slew thousands and carried other thousands into captivity for the next seventy years. Let the prophet Jeremiah tell you why: *To fulfil the word of the Lord by the mouth of Jeremiah, until the land had enjoyed her sabbaths: for as long as she lay desolate she kept sabbath, to fulfill threescore and ten years.* (2 Chronicles 36:21)

How exact is God's judgment for violating His laws about the Sabbath? When they entered the land God deeded to them, He told them to let the land lay idle every seventh year and He would supply their needs. They never obeyed. In 586 B.C. they had been in the land 490 years –seventy Sabbaths. God collected all of them at one time. Don't count on prospering by disobeying God. Friend, you don't want to live where the Lord's Day is abused? Better still, if you want to be a godly and effective Christian, consider the following from two great Puritans from the past:

> "There are no Christians in all the world comparable for power of godliness and heights of grace, holiness, and communion with God, to those who are more strict, serious, studious and conscientious in sanctifying the Lord's day...True reason why the power of godliness is fallen to so low an ebb, both in this and in other countries is because the Sabbath is no longer strictly and conscientiously observed...And O that all these short hints might be so blessed from heaven as to work us all to a more strict seriousness and conscientious sanctifying of the Lord's Day."
> --(Thomas Brooks (1608 – 1680)[16]

> "I have found that by a strict and diligent

observation that a due observance of the duties of the Lord's Day hath ever had joined to it a blessing upon the rest of my time, and the week that hath been so begun hath been blessed and prosperous to me; and on the other side, when I have been negligent of the day, the rest of the week has been unsuccessful and unhappy in my own secular employments. This I write, not lightly or inconsiderately, but upon long and sound observation and experience."

--(Sir Matthew Hale 1609)[17]

Consider God's Precious Promise to Those Who Honor His Day.

If thou turn away thy foot from the sabbath, from doing thy pleasure on my holy day; and call the sabbath a delight, the holy of the Lord, honourable; and shalt honour him, not doing thine own ways, nor finding thine own pleasure, nor speaking thine own words: Then shalt thou delight thyself in the Lord; and I will cause thee to ride upon the high places of the earth, and feed thee with the heritage of Jacob thy father: for the mouth of the Lord hath spoken it. (Isaiah 58:13-14)

The opposite is in store for all who dishonor His Day. The choice is yours.

Chapter Eleven

Music And Musicians

Known for their singing, the Babylonian captors of the Jews asked them to *Sing us one of the songs of Zion.* (Psalm 137:3) Their response was *How shall we sing the Lord's song in a foreign land?* (137:4) Regarding the kind of music in many churches today, someone has quipped, "How shall we sing a foreign song in the Lord's land?"

Today's Contemporary Christian Music is indeed "foreign" to the godly and scripturally informed followers of our Lord. It is the off-shoot of the Rock and Roll born in the '50's of unsavory characters whose lifestyle true believers would not consider born-again children of a holy God. Few would argue that there would ever have been "Christian Rock" (a serious misnomer) had there not first been Rock and Roll.

Soon sweeping the world with such groups as the Beatles and the name of Elvis Presley, the loud, lustful, liberating (to the flesh) beat and lyrics of Rock and Roll were drastically changing an entire generation of young people while shocking their parents and grandparents. As a teenage ministerial student in Bible College in those days, I felt something was wrong with this music. Although slow in coming, with the help of some older preachers, I came to the conclusion, there was a lot wrong with it and it has gotten a lot worse.

Through these years, I have continued to study this "music" (?) and the horrible effects of Rock and Roll. Now a grandparent, indeed a great grandparent, having seen and studied the Rock and Roll culture and its consequences on our country and churches, as a pastor for forty years and working with hundreds of young people in our Christian School for thirty years, as a servant of my Savior, I feel compelled to cry out against this unholy plague.

After dealing with the corrupt nature of secular Rock and Roll, we will look at how it then linked with religious music to form Contemporary Christian Music (CCM) that has wrought such havoc and destruction to the work of God. First, understand

Rock and Roll Is The Music of Rebels

It is rebellion against all authority—parental, police, government, preachers, churches, the Bible and the God of the Bible. Those involved in it are on record as admitting—yes, bragging that this is true. Consider a couple of samples:

In the popular book *Blue Like Jazz,* Donald Miller tells how he had refused to be restricted by the teaching of traditional-type churches. He wanted to drink beer and watch raunchy movies and talk trashy and run around with atheists and other rebels. Now, with his emerging CCM stance, he can do that. At a book signing for *Blue Like Jazz,* a young woman who had purchased multiple copies said, "I'm a Jesus girl, but I also like to go out and do tequila shots with my friends. This is a book I can give to them.

"In *A Renegade's Guide to God*, David Foster mocks "Bible thumpers" and calls for a "renegade" type of Christianity that "resists being named, revolts at being shamed, and rebels against being tamed" (p. 8). He says, "We won't be 'told' what to do or 'commanded' how to behave." (p. 10)[18]

Though this is evident in their music, those few who dare to point this out and say it is wrong and destructive, especially to our youth will tell you expect to be labeled a "legalist," a "Pharisee" or something much worse.

Rock and Roll is Sexual

Again, hear it from the Rock and Roll Musicians themselves. Scores of quotes to support this could be listed. Here are a few samples. The dates go away back, but things have not changed, except to get worse.

> "That's what rock is all about--sex with a 100 megaton bomb, the beat!" (Gene Simmons of the rock group Kiss, interview,

> "Rock 'n' roll is 99% sex" (John Oates of the rock duo Hall Oates)

> "Listen, rock 'n roll AIN'T CHURCH. It's nasty business..." (Lita Ford of heavy metal group The 'Rock' is the total celebration of the physical" (Ted Nugent, rock star).

> "Rock music is sex. The big beat matches the body's rhythms" (Frank Zappa of the Mothers of Invention.)[19]

From its inception, the very name "Rock and Roll" has been seen as a euphemism for partying and fornication. Those who know music well and are familiar with the different kinds of beats and how they affect the body can tell you they break down a person's resistance, send them moving, and how it then leads to serious problems.

How can music that has always been acclaimed by the world as sexual, all of a sudden become spiritual through the addition of some Christian words?

Rock and Roll Is Violent

Violent to the extreme! Advocating killing the police who protect them and even their parents who love and support them. Rap is especially violent. As I write this, a major item in the news is the horrific story of a USA newsman having been beheaded by a member of the terrorist organization ISIS. It was carried out on camera. The report is now saying the murderer was probably from England and was a former rapper who had been radicalized. Consider the following cases:

"King Tubby, who invented the dubbing process that was popularized by rappers, was murdered in 1989 when he was 58 years old.

"Trouble T-Roy (Troy Dixon), rapper with Heavy D and the Boyz, fell off a balcony after a concert in 1990 at age 22.

"Eazy-E (Eric Wright) of N.W.A., one of the founders of Gangsta rap, died of AIDS in 1995 at age 31. His lyrics focused on themes such as guns, drugs, anti-law enforcement, and deviant sex. He had seven children by six different women.

"Mr. Cee, rapper with R.B.L. Posse (Ruthless By Law), died after being shot nine times on New Year's morning of 1996 at about age 30."[20]

The list goes on and on. God's law of reaping what you sow (Galatians 6:7-8) is certainly seen in this foul industry.

Rock and Roll Music Is a "Drug"

Rock and Roll and the drug culture have been locked together since the 50's. A glance at what is happening in Colorado recently since they legalized the sale of marijuana is proof they still are. But along with the "weed," consider the music itself. Listen to Janis Joplin tell of her experience when she attended her first big rock concert:

> "I couldn't believe it, all that rhythm and power. I got stoned just feeling it, like IT WAS THE BEST DOPE IN THE WORLD. It was SO SENSUAL, so vibrant, loud, crazy."
> --(Joel Dreyfuss, *Witchita* Eagle, 10-6-1970)[21]

> "A 2012 study by the University of Washington concluded that mega churches 'provide the same biological 'high' and euphoria as that produced by sporting events and concerts...The study, entitled 'God Is Like a Drug:' was co-authored by Katie Corcoran and James Wellman. They attribute the worship 'high' to the 'upbeat' modern music, cameras that scan the audience and project smiling, dancing, singing, or crying worshippers on large screens, and an extremely charismatic leader whose sermons touch individuals on an emotional level.' They believe these things 'trigger chemicals in the brain to give the individual an emotional 'high' and feeling of transcendence as well as a need to come back for another 'hit.'"[22]

'Timothy Leary, the '60s LSD guru, who was an expert both in drugs and in rock music, testified: 'Don't listen to the words, it's the music that has its own message. ... I've been STONED ON THE MUSIC many times' (Politics of Ecstasy, 1968). He was right, of course, about the hypnotic, addictive, incredibly sensual power of rock and roll. And notice that he IS NOT TALKING ABOUT THE WORDS, but of the music itself, of the rhythm, the backbeat, the heavy relentless syncopation.

"Steven Tyler of Aerosmith said, "[Rock music] is the strongest drug in the world."[23]

Let me add, like drugs, those you start off with the milder drugs, more often than not, move on to the stronger ones to get the same or stronger high. The same is true of this music. Feeding the flock the "soft rock" at church entices them to seek the real rock at home and in cars.

From Rock and Roll to "Christian" Rock and CCM

Early in my studies of the Scriptures, I wondered how all the various religions, with their many doctrinal differences and traditions would ever be brought into one organization--the one-world harlot church of Revelation 17. When the self-proclaimed higher critics from Europe invaded the seminaries of America, the result was they produced modernistic ministers who were "too intelligent" (their own estimate) to believe the Bible was true. Such preachers in the pulpits soon poisoned the mainline denominations. Since they were now agreed in their unbelief, there was now little difference in their denominations.

As a rule, the churches in these liberal denominations began to dry up. Soon the mid-week service was dropped, then Sunday nights, and certainly, no revivals were scheduled to try to revive the church and win souls. Their common denominator was a social gospel of helping people in this world with little if any thought of eternity. The churches that were growing were those that preached the saving gospel of Jesus Christ. Their pastors were not the products of the liberal seminaries. Instead, many of them were from recently founded fundamental Bible Colleges, often with only a three-year course of study. More were self-taught or only received some training in Bible Institutes.

As a whole, these men had grasped the truth of the Word of God, believed it fully, and were committed to preaching it. I wondered how these men, and the churches they were building, could ever be lured into an apostate conglomerate that would be called a church. We now know the answer. The Satanic tool this time would not be intellectualism from the highly degreed higher critics. Whether or not the Bible was true would not be the issue. Instead, it, with its divine authority, would be basically ignored, replaced by a movement of emotion and feelings suited to man's fallen flesh.

First, those churches, founded on inspired truth and clear on the gospel, had to be lulled to sleep in a lukewarm, materialistic, self-satisfied atmosphere. (Compare the Laodicean church in Revelation 3.) Soul winning revivals had to be reduced from 2-3 weeks to, at the most, four days, and then cancelled completely. Preaching on the great doctrines like the atoning death of Jesus Christ and the necessity of repentance of sin (and naming it) had to be abandoned along with everything negative. The services became brief, boring, and doomed unless something changed.

> Today many churches have made entertainment the big deal.

Two things changed that influenced the situation:

(1) **Rock and Roll stormed on to the scene**. It was wild, emotional, captivating as the performers threw everything into what they were doing.

(2) **The Pentecostal/Charismatic movement,** that had been on the scene for about fifty years with only minimal growth, began to move toward the style of the music of the rockers.

They didn't have far to go. Both were very emotional with lots of physical movement—jumping, falling, rolling, etc. Both were loud, used similar kinds of instruments, and followed their feelings rather than rational thinking or the inerrant Word of God. Both groups created something of an atmosphere of mindlessness. As a movement, the Charismatics have not been a biblically, scholarly movement. They are prone to push the authority of the Scriptures aside, putting experience and their erroneous teaching on speaking in tongues in its place. They claim God is speaking through them. If the latter is so, then it would have to be true and on par with the Bible. So they are adding to the Scriptures and often contradicting it. That is similar to the claims of Roman Catholic Popes when they claim to be speaking Ex cathedra.

In the sixties, the Charismatic movement mushroomed! Denominations like the Assembly of God drew huge crowds, built large churches, and impacted and attracted many from the dying, mainline denominations including many Roman Catholics. The movement was labeled "Wildfire" by many and drew a response from those joining it, "I'd rather have 'wildfire' than no fire.'" The beat of their music merged with the rockers more and more, luring in many who were hooked on that kind of music from the world.

There was no denying the movement was changing the religious landscape in America and even overseas. The Full Gospel Businessmen's organization operated outside church walls and impacted many men of means from mainline churches and again, many Catholics. They were received as full brothers if they had spoken in tongues regardless of what heresies they might believe. They gained the attention and acceptance of the Pope and some of their leaders were invited to visit the Vatican. Soon they sponsored a huge Charismatic conference on the campus of Notre Dame University, the center of Catholicism in America. I read years ago that 25% of all practicing Catholics in the USA had spoken in tongues.

The great growth of the charismatic churches (which usually claim to be non-denominational and the name over the door told you nothing) was a challenge to other churches. Soon you found Presbyterian, Methodist, Lutheran, and Baptist churches, etc. imitating the example of these growing congregations. It was not uncommon, not only to hear the big beat coming from these churches, but to see outdoor stages for their bands during the warm days of summer where night services carried the same sounds.

> **Today, too many churches have made entertainment the big deal. They've forgotten the people are there to be fed, not entertained. (I am not saying that entertainment has no place in a church.)**
>
> **Their argument, of course, is that "if we don't have a music program that appeals to the young people, we'll loose them."**
>
> **It's a powerful argument, actually. But, it is also a flawed argument because it presupposes that the way to keep the young people in the church is to give them music that satisfies their culturally-induced appetites and that there are no alternatives.**[24]

Numerous organizations sprang up to help you market your church. Conferences on Church Growth became common. Pastors often received literature urging them to attend them or invite their representatives to come to their church, assuring them this would greatly increase their attendance. All of that was for a price. Books were written on the subject. Religious pollsters, like George Barna published the kind of program he thought a church needed to follow to draw the crowds. According to Barna, who holds a broad view of who are Christians, including such cults as Mormons, advised that the first twenty minutes of the church service should be uninterrupted music and the sermon must be brief, not over twenty minutes if I rightly recall.

Soon mega-churches were popping up all over the country. Mostly their names (sometimes just changed from what denomination they were) were generic, but their music was all alike. Not evident from their names, but most of them were charismatic or at least tolerant of those teachings. As the big-beat music gained in popularity, it soon became the main thing on the menu in Baptist churches as well as others.

Worship leaders (no longer music directors or song leaders) who were talented in the new music were much in demand and soon found themselves on church payrolls. Small groups formed who had vocal and/or instrumental talents. They did concerts, made recordings--and money! At their concerts, apart from the words, it was difficult to distinguish them from the usual rock concerts. They dressed and sounded the same. Contemporary "Christian" Music had arrived and Lucifer, the fallen Master of Music from heaven had a new weapon to use against Christ's Church.

Something had gone seriously wrong in the Lord's House because,

Preaching, Not Music,
is the Center in New Testament Christianity!

- *It pleased God by the foolishness of preaching to save them that believe.* (1 Corinthians 1:21)

- Three thousand souls were saved on Pentecost, the birthday of the church when the gospel was preached in the power of the Holy Spirit. (Acts 2) There was no music.

That is not to say there is not to be music in our church services. Scripture sanctions the use of music and tells us what kind it needs to be and that it must come from a life filled with the Spirit (Ephesians 5:18-19). But preaching, not music, is to be the center of the service.

That has been so in the Lord's Church through the centuries. You could usually tell that was so when you entered the church building. The pulpit—the place from which to the Word of God was preached—was in the center. In some churches there is a place for the preacher at one side and another place (usually smaller) on the other side. The communion table is in the center. Such an arrangement is called a "divided chancel."

All of that was symbolic. What was in the center was considered to be the main thing. Was it taking communion or preaching? In RC Churches, it is the partaking of the elements of communion at what they call the Mass. They are not the only ones who practice that. That is not how it should be in the New Testament church. But does it matter?

If you could ask Moses if it made any difference whether or not he followed the pattern God gave him for building the Tabernacle, he would have said, he was told repeatedly to be sure he followed God's pattern: *Moses was admonished of God when he was about to make the tabernacle: for, See, saith he, that thou make all things according to the pattern shewed to thee in the mount.* (Hebrews 8:5)

Every detail in the Tabernacle was divinely designed to point to Jesus. It was now at this place God promised to meet with His people and dwell with them. (Exodus 25:8, 22) The bodies of individual believers are temples of the Holy Spirit (1 Corinthians 6:13), but the church collectively is also the temple, the dwelling place of God. (1 Corinthians 3:16).

Someone has said "The church is the window through which the world sees who Jesus is and learns what the gospel is." Change from what was ordained and, as was the case in the church at Corinth over speaking in tongues, unbelievers *"will they not say that ye are mad* [crazy]?" (1 Corinthians 14:23). Conversely, if prophesy (preaching) is done and there is order in the service, the secrets of the unsaved hearts are made manifest; *and so falling down on his face he will worship God and report that God is in you of a truth.* (1 Corinthians 14:25)

In summary, the points are these: Music—any kind of music--is not to be the main thing in the church service. The preaching of God's Word is to have the preeminent place. Secondly, bringing in unholy, carnal music, born in the ungodly world and brought into God's church by worldly and often heretical people has no place in the worship of the thrice holy God!

"Billy Graham went worldwide April 14 with an MTV-style telecast aimed at a young audience. This largest-audience-ever telecast used music from Nirvana, whose lead singer Kurt Cobain committed suicide. It used two dramatic films featuring DC Talk and messages from liberal Andrew Young and Glen Campbell. Graham has reoriented his crusades the past two years, and now his TV ministry, to attract a younger audience."[25]

Is Music Neutral?

Those who defend Contemporary Christian Music often argue that the only things that matter are that the words are Christian and whether or not the musicians are sincere.

The Following statements by CCM defenders:

"Music is not good or evil because of the formation of the notes or the structure of the beat. Music is good because the heart of the person playing it is innocently and sincerely giving praise to our God"
--(Mylon LeFevre, interview by Pastor Rick Anderson, Minneapolis, Minnesota,

"...we need to stop advocating one music style over against another. Our tradition, our style, our renderings have to do with ourselves, not with God."
--Anthony Gentes, *The Worship Thought*, July 2003.

"There is no such thing as 'gospel music.' Every style and form of music can become gospel, whether it's jazz, pop, rock 'n' roll, or rap." --*Don Butler, Gospel Music Association*

"There is no style of music that can't be enjoyed by Christians." -- *Ralph Carmichael*

"God speaks through all different kinds of musical styles" –Bill Gaither[26]

This writer is not a musician (though many in my family are), but you don't have to be a musician to know the above claims are false. If you know what the Bible says about music, what kind of music has characterized the history of the Lord's church throughout the centuries and especially during times of great revivals where so many of the great hymns were born, you can readily distinguish between the CCM music and what Paul said about music in Ephesians 5:19: *Speaking to yourselves in psalms and hymns and spiritual songs, singing and making melody in your heart to the Lord.* Can you imagine a tavern owner playing godly hymns? It would ruin his business. Bringing his music into the church will also ruin the churches.

Many congregations have split over this new music in recent years, more than over any other issue. Study the lives of those who go with the traditional music in contrast to those who follow the CCM crowd. Yes, they usually have the crowd. But even that tells you something worth noting.

If all music is amoral, consider the following:

Why does the movie industry use different styles of music along with the visuals to create different emotions?

Why do the night clubs all play a certain kind of music?

How is it, as mentioned above, the rock musicians claim their heavily syncopated rhythm is sexy? How can this music, from those who created it, be called sexual, suddenly become spiritual by adding a few Christian words that are basically drowned out by the beat?

From my own experience, I share the following. Anyone familiar with the voodoo music from Africa or Haiti can tell you all music is not amoral. I have been exposed to it in both places. (In Haiti 28 times between 1999 and 2011 and in Africa in 1971.)

I didn't at first believe what I was told happens each year in Haiti when 200,000 to 250,000 gather at a beautiful waterfall to celebrate Satan's birthday. Voodoo priests from across the island gather there and several hundred young virgin Haitian girls are brought in. When the drum beat begins and the girls begin to dance and the beat gets faster and louder, until the girls begin to collapse, and the voodoo priests move in---What follows is too vile for descent minds to ponder. I have been to that waterfall and talked with missionaries that have assured me what I had been told was true. I asked, "What happens to those girls?" "They then belong to that voodoo priest. They never marry. Some of the priests have as many as thirty of these girls."

Regarding that demonic beat, a young navy man in our church, who had been deep into Rock 'n Roll before his conversion to Christ, told me some of the most famous names in the Rock 'n Roll crowd go to Haiti to try to learn to imitate that beat. He named one of them he knew who had been there.

Many Bible students believe Satan, before his rebellion and eviction from heaven, was a great musician. In his hatred of our holy God, he has corrupted everything he can. If he has failed to corrupt music, he has missed a great opportunity to hurt and hinder God's work. He is not that dumb.

Well respected in the field of Christian music, regarding CCM music being amoral and suitable if he musicians are sincere, Dr. Frank Garlock wrote, "Sincerity and motivation have never been a test of real spirituality or even of Christianity for that matter. The Word of God is that which will abide forever, and it is upon His Word that God hinges all spiritual truth. It is not right to ignore the Bible, to become worldly in philosophy and practice, to call things Christian which are not, nor to disobey the Word of God, even to try to win people to Christ."[27]

Evangelist Gordon Sears added this observation to the above: "When the standard of music is LOWERED, then the standard of dress is also lowered. When the standard of dress is lowered, then the standard of conduct is also lowered. When the standard of conduct is lowered, then the sense of value in God's truth is lowered."[28]

We are to test music by the Word of God. It doesn't matter what you like or dislike, but what is acceptable to God. The CCM movement says that music is amoral, which means that God doesn't care one way or another. God does care (Isaiah 5:20). God wants you to have discernment in every area of your life. One of these areas is music.

Question: If rock music is necessary or even important for the service and worship of Christ, what did God's people do in ages past?

They didn't have the kind of instruments to produce the music that blast our ears like what is produced today. To be sure, the pagan came up with something that pleased and excited the flesh, but God didn't accept it then nor will He now. The holy God of heaven has told us the kind of music He accepts and it is not the kind offered to the idols like the pagans did then and CCM is doing today. He is a Jealous God and will not share His worship with the idols of this world.

From my reading over many years, I have learned that so many of these contemporary Christian musicians love secular rock and are wrapped up in it. They listen to it in their private lives and they perform it in their concerts and record it for their albums. They even use secular rock in the worship of God. The thrice holy God of heaven will not have it nor should we!

CCM –The Musicians

One of the things that screams at us regarding CCM music is that it is not fit for the worship of our holy God because of the unfitness of the musicians! In this age of almost unlimited information at our fingertips, it is easy to know who these musicians are, how they live, and what they believe. We marvel at how naive congregations adopt the music without knowing anything about the people who wrote the songs or those performing them. Congregations, searching for a pastor, who would insist that the pulpit committee thoroughly check out any candidate before they recommend him to their church, yet, when it comes to their music, it is another matter. We believe the Holy Bible requires, not only those who preach the Word to live holy lives, but also all of those who purport to minister to us in other areas do the same. That includes the musicians. Tainted Talent is a curse to the church of Jesus Christ.

Before referencing famous names, allow me to speak of a case with which I am familiar. A large church in our area has a man on the stage on Sunday's who plays music in night clubs on Saturday nights, is living with a woman to whom he is not married, invited a number of people from his church to a party at his house and served them beer. One of the pastoral staff attended. If you want to know what Paul would have done and said any church should do is such a case, read what he wrote under the Holy Spirit's inspiration in 1 Corinthians 5. I will spare you the time. Repeatedly he said, he must be "taken away," (excommunicated), "delivered to Satan", "purge[d] out," and not to have any fellowship with him. (Verses 2, 5, 7, 9-11)

In light of that, ponder the popularity of some famous names from CCM who have admitted various serious sins and continue in the limelight:

> "CCM singer Michael English, gospel music's artist of the year, left The Gaither Vocal Band in April. Then in May, he returned his six Dove awards after confessing to an adulterous affair with another CCM performer, First Call's Marabeth Jordon, is now expecting his child (5/21 *World*). This is a wake-up call, and may just

be the tip of a long-rumored scandal-ridden "gospel" entertainer iceburg. English, citing human failings, quits as a Christian singer, but may pursue plans with Bill Gaither to form a new record label. (5/6 H.T.). The Gospel Music Association says he can have his awards back anytime he wants them."[29]

"The members of the Christian rock band Stryper admitted today that they drank and partied in carnal rebellion during part of their touring career. Michael English, Sandi Patty, Kirk Franklin, among others, admits that they were living in fornication and adultery during part of their careers. Mylon LeFevre admits that he wrote and performed music for years before he got right with God, and that he was using drugs heavily and drinking and carousing even while producing Christian music.

"Many CCM spokesmen have honestly admitted that this type of thing is a big problem in their midst. Often, it is covered up to protect the careers of the worldly musicians and to protect the reputation and financial bottom line of the CCM industry. You probably know that CCM music is a huge business. However, you may be surprised to learn secular companies own most of this industry. WORD ENTERTAINMENT, a secular company, is the home of many of the big names in CCM."[30]

The first impression of godly believers about the CCM musicians is usually their appearance and their style of dress. Both the men and the women, by design, are dressed like the world's rock and roll groups. They have subscribed to the idea that to win the world we need to be like the world. So the women wear the revealing, provocative styles like the world. The men have the long, shaggy, and punk hair of the world and both sexes have body piercing and the tattoos (forbidden in Leviticus 19:28 NKJV) and/or earrings and anything else that imitates the world.

Consider three categories of sin that are widespread among CCM people.

(1) The sin of sodomy: We could give a catalog of various sins, but this one has been chosen because most people would not associate it with anything Christian. But such is not the case. All who know scripture know the holy God of the Holy Bible names and condemns this sin in no uncertain terms in both the Old Testament and the New. In Leviticus 19:22, God says *Thou shalt not lie with mankind as with womankind; it is **abomination.*** (Leviticus 19:22) In the Romans 1:27, God condemns this sin in both sexes when he had Paul write, *And likewise also the men, leaving the natural use of the woman, burned in their lust one toward another; men with men working that which is unseemly, and receiving in themselves that recompense of their error which was meet.* In Genesis 19, God "poured hell out of heaven" (Charles Spurgeon) on the cities of Sodom and Gomorrah because of this sin. The sin of sodomy gets its name from that city. Many defend it. Others admit being involved in it. Weep as you read the following paragraphs:

> "In 2014, Dan Haseltine, front man for the popular and influential CCM band Jars of Clay, announced his support for 'gay marriage'" He wrote the following in a series of Twitter posts: 'Not meaning to stir things up BUT... is there a non-speculative or non-slippery slope' reason why gays shouldn't marry? I don't hear one. ... I'm trying to make sense of the conservative argument. But it doesn't hold up to basic scrutiny.
>
> "In The Gospel Sound, which first

appeared in 1971, Anthony Heilbut said, "The gospel church has long been a refuge for gays and lesbians, some of whom grew up to be among the greatest singers and musicians." Douglas Harrison, a homosexual who grew up Southern Baptist, said,... 'you can't swing a Dove Award without hitting upon evidence of the longstanding, deep-set presence of queer experience in, and its influence on, Christian music culture at all levels' ('Come Out from among Them,' Religion Dispatches, April 30, 2010). In 1998, CCM star Kirk Franklin said that 'homosexuality ... is a problem today in gospel music--a MAJOR CONCERN—and everybody knows it' ...James Cleveland, who has been called the 'King of Gospel,' was a homosexual who died of AIDS.

"Marsha Stevens, author of the popular song 'For Those Tears I Died (Come to the Water)' co-founded Children of the Day, one of the first Contemporary Christian Music groups associated with Calvary Chapel. In 1979, Marsha broke her sacred marriage vows and divorced her husband of seven years, with whom she had two children, because she had 'fallen in love with a woman.' Eventually Marsha 'married' Cindi Stevens-Pino who she calls 'my wife'. She started her own label called BALM (Born Again Lesbian Music) and performs between 150 and 200 concerts a year. She has a program called 'upBeat' through which she produces a praise and worship album annually with a variety of singers and songwriters.

"In June, 2013, popular CCM Sandi Patty

performed with the homosexual Turtle Creek Chorale at the Meyerson Symphony Center in Dallas, Texas. On July 2012, the Chorale attended the Gay and Lesbian Association of Choruses (GALA in Denver ('Turtle Creek Chorale's 2012-2013 Season,' Turtlecreek.org).

"Other homosexual CCM artists are Anthony Williams , Kirk Talley, Clay Aiken, Doug Pinnock of King's X, Amy Ray and Emily Saliers of Indigo Girls, and Jennifer Knapp."[31]

The above is only a small sampling. This should not be shocking to true believers when you realize these musicians have been viewed as Christians simply because that is what they call themselves, although their lives fail to back up that claim. I cannot find his actual quote, (remember it was in CN) but I recall reading several years go a statement by Tony Campolo, who is nowhere near the conservative camp of believers. He was often a speaker at the big outdoor rallies of so-called Christian Rock. He mentioned how they would go on stage and says things like "Let's hear it for Jesus," but backstage, it was scary!

So if you want to know what is wrong with CCM music, begin by checking out the lifestyle of the musicians. It is easy to find this out in this information age. But secondly,

(2) The Ecumenical Aims of CCM: Years ago I heard Doug Oldham, featured singer on Jerry Falwell's TV program, say he could go anywhere with his music. It brought people together. But doctrine (the word means teaching, truth)—doctrine divides. To the degree that was true four decades ago, it is many times worse today. Many of the CCM musicians are on record as saying they hope their music will bring all "Christians" together. By "Christians," they mean everyone who claims to believe anything about Jesus, whether it is the Jesus of the Bible or not. The most radical would even include other religions. Their quotes below will reveal this. By doing so, they fit right in with what has become the religion of America and much of the world. That is the idea that all religions, if seriously followed, will get you to heaven. Untouchables like Evangelist Billy Graham agree with that. For himself, he simply says he has chosen Jesus, believing He is the best way, but not the only way. How do you square that with John 14:6?

Serious students of the Scriptures and the times in which we live have watched the <u>ecumenical movement</u> mushroom in recent years. The word means universal, or unity, and the design of the movement is to achieve universal religious unity. Again, their definition of Christianity is at odds with scripture. They are fond of the phrase in John 17:21, *that they all may be one,* (which they misinterpret), but have chosen to ignore and violate the truth stated so clearly in passages like Romans 16:17. *Now I beseech you, brethren, mark them which cause divisions and offences contrary to the doctrine which ye have learned; and avoid them.* Those "divisions and offences" may be over doctrine or, as we shall show here, caused by such things as CCM music.

First, we need to know that God's Word tells us clearly that there is going to be a one-world church at the end of this age. In contrast to the true church, Jesus' pure bride, the one for which He died, this coming ecumenical church will be a harlot. Revelation 17:1, 2 refers to it as *"the great whore that sitteth upon many waters [peoples, verse 15.] with whom the kings of the earth have committed fornication and the inhabitants of the earth have been made drunk with the wine of her fornication."* God's Word warns us, *Come out of her, my people, that ye be not partakers of her sins, and that ye receive not of her plagues.* (Revelation 18:4)

We have previously mentioned how pseudo-intellectualism and philosophy from Europe invaded the seminaries in the 1800's, attacking the integrity of the inspired Word of God, and bringing about a unity among many mainline denominations. Then, in the mid-nineteen hundreds, myriads of emotional, ill-informed charismatic's, with their fanatical emphasis on their unscriptural teaching on speaking in *"unknown"* (not in the original text) tongues, while ignoring key doctrines, have united many other groups. Together, they have greatly aided the creation of the religion that dominates America today, the idea that you can believe what you want to, be a part of any religion and any of them will get you to heaven.

> **The ecumenical philosophy is the theme song of Contemporary Christian Music.**

There have been many events that stand out to those of us who have followed this unholy alliance during the past fifty years. One event that I believe should open the eyes of ordinary lay people was the call to prayer arranged by President Bush only hours after the attack on 911. It took place in the Washington National Cathedral. The religious representatives were Evangelist Billy Graham, a Jewish Rabbi, a Roman Catholic Priest, and a Muslim Cleric.

The intended lesson is inescapable. All religions are the same. All have equal access to God—whoever God is. That is what President Bush apparently believes (as do most Americans), and what he was conveying. The same was/is true of Billy Graham. That is overwhelmingly what America believes. That is a clear manifestation of the ecumenical movement. It is a blatant denial of Jesus' statement in John 14:6, "I am the way, the truth, and the life: no man cometh unto the Father, but by me." It makes a mockery of Jesus as a dying Savior of sinners and puts all man-made efforts on the same level as His sacrificial death in our behalf. But that is the religion of the majority of Americans and many other countries. The way to be popular is to be in step with that and help bring it about. That is where many, indeed the majority of CCM musicians are. Their music, more than anything else, is what is bringing all religions together today.

The greatest danger in dabbling with contemporary praise music is the fact that it is a bridge to the end-time one-world church.

Consider Canadian born Matt Maher, a popular contemporary worship musician. He ministers at Our Lady of Mount Carmel Parish in Tempe, Arizona, which is devoted to Mary as the Queen of Heaven. The sign at the front of the church says, "Mary, Mother of Life, pray for us."

He calls himself a "musical missionary," a missionary for Rome, that is.

Maher, who tours with non-Catholics, comments:

"What's fantastic about it is we're all Christians from different denominations and we're learning to understand each other. It just means that we're writing about mysteries that we don't fully understand." He sees his music as a "bridge." He says that contemporary worship music is a way to "build relationships with people and link arms with them for the Kingdom." He says that touring with people like Michael W. Smith is producing ecumenical unity, because people come to the concerts and find themselves standing beside a priest or nun and they learn that "we're all in this family together."[32]

We ask "What family?" And "What kingdom?"

Maher insisted that the problem in getting all churches together with Roman Catholics is that people do not understand the Catholic teaching. That is not true. He is the one who is deceived. I have books written and printed by the Roman Catholics, explaining their doctrine and have studied and written about it for years. Anyone who thinks they believe "Salvation is by grace alone, through faith alone, in Christ alone" (the motto of the Great Reformation), needs to read their response to that at the Council of Trent (1545-1563). Here is some of what they said then:

> **Face It!**
>
> **CCM Music was NOT birthed by godly, biblical people.**

"If anyone says that justifying faith is nothing else than confidence in divine mercy, which remits sins for Christ's sake, or that it is this confidence alone that justifies us, LET HIM BE ANATHEMA [accursed]" (Sixth Session, Canons Concerning Justification, Canon 12). This has never been changed, but is still the position of Rome today!

When the *Promise Keepers* movement appeared on the American religious scene a few years ago, they adopted that great statement regarding salvation, the *Sola Scriptura* of the Reformation. The Roman Catholics participated in *Promise Keepers*, but only after they got that statement changed. They would not tolerate the statement that salvation is through Christ alone. They insist salvation must include coming through the Roman Catholic Church. Maher is one of many CCM musicians who is reversing what was accomplished by the Great Protestant Reformation.

The charismatics have been in the forefront of the CCM movement. Anyone who has been to any of their big conferences knows that they are totally ecumenical. Denominations of all descriptions are present and represented by their leaders and their musicians. The heresies they teach that cost people their souls are not exposed. Associations like the New Baptist Covenant Celebration of 2008 revealed the same ecumenical position. What else would you expect from speakers like Jimmy Carter, Al Gore, Tony Campolo, and Bill Clinton?

David Cloud has attended many of these conferences for years. (See his resume in the "Endnotes") The following are some of his observations from one such meeting:

> "I attended the National Pastor's Fellowship in 2009 sponsored by Zondervan and InterVarsity Press with speakers such as Brian McLaren, Bill Hybels, Paul Young, author of *The Shack.*

> "The music at these forums was 'real' Christian rock. They pulled out all the stops. No messing around with this silly business of trying to remove 'the rock' from Christian rock. There was even colored lights and smoke. No holds barred CCM. The real stuff.

> "All of these large influential conferences are committed to the ecumenical philosophy. None of them would dream of reproving Roman Catholicism. They are far too busy with other agendas to do anything like that. These conferences throw men together of all doctrinal persuasions, from Leighton Ford's' 'evangelical conservatism' to Brian McLaren's universalism and rejection of hell to Paul Young's non-

judgmental female God as taught in his book *The Shack.*

"These are the types of forums in which CCM is birthed and where it is most at home.

He added this in an interview with *Christianity Today,* Don Moen of Integrity Music said: "I've discovered that worship [music] is Trans-denominational, transcultural. IT BRIDGES ANY DENOMINATION."[33]

When Elvis Presley and the Beatles catapulted to the top of the charts back in the '50's, I recall being shocked by what their music was doing to society, especially the youth. Anyone with a smidgen of Christianity could tell this was the flesh let loose. I was shocked when that same beat—the beat that brings out the beast rather than the best—would be allowed in churches, especially Bible-believing churches. I recall the first time I heard that music coming from a supposedly Christian service. I was in Nashville, Tennessee driving my 1960 VW to the church I pastored when I heard this wild music! It was coming from a tent revival service up on a knoll next to me. I could not see the tent, but you couldn't keep from hearing the sound. I literally hit the brakes and stopped in the middle of a main street!

When the famous "healing" Evangelist, Oral Roberts, from my home state of Oklahoma, added ill-clad females on stage doing their "choreography" I thought surely he would loose his Pentecostal (holiness) base. I was wrong. That beat, regardless of the words or the claims of the musicians, moves the body and today we are witnessing uninhibited abandon to that beat from those in the audience as well as those on the stage.

Those in churches who cared asked, "How can this be happening?" The answer is incriminating. Genuine revivals had become a thing of the past. There was no longer a revivalist in America recognized and respected for preaching against sin. The Bible Colleges and Seminaries, like the churches, had lost their fire. Truth that was taught was more often than not, done by professionals that did it nonchalantly, who managed to convey it only to heads and not to hearts. Standards of holiness dropped. So did attendance at Sunday and Wednesday night services until both were eventually discontinued.

The churches that grew had gifted leaders who were more CEO's and administrators than pastors or preachers. Their "ministry" (or their ego) was too big for them to go soul winning, so they hired help to do the visiting and musicians to give the carnal congregations (often comprised of mainly unsaved members) the kind of music their flesh wanted to lure in the crowds.

An example of that was several years ago, Rick Warren, pastor of Saddleback Church, Lake Forest, CA, one of the largest churches in the nation, passed out cards to his congregation and asked them to list what radio stations they listened to. Overwhelmingly, they were rock and roll stations. He decided to give them what they wanted.

Today, you can go to churches of varied religious traditions and basically hear the same music. It may be toned down and somewhat adapted, but it is still the same rock beat. This music is what lures them in, creates a unity of churches—a unity that, regardless what they disagree on, they believe in and are going along with the ecumenical movement to bring all churches together. The writers and performers of that music are committed to bringing all churches together. They have already succeeded in quickly bringing many of them into what will evolve into that one-world harlot church. In the meantime, they are admittedly targeting the churches that are Bible-based, use the old hymns, and have services like God's people have done for centuries.

The CCM musicians committed to the ecumenical philosophy use so-called "bridge songs" to gain this end. The lyrics of these songs are true to scripture and, though the beat is basically the same, it is greatly toned down. This is the "bait" to lure traditional churches into their camp. Undiscerning leaders are not apt to detect this bait and feel such songs are safe. Such songs as "How Deep the Father's Love for Us" by Stuart Townend and "In Christ Alone" by Townend and Keith Getty are examples of bridge songs. Some of those hearing these songs in their traditional churches will find more such songs in Christian Bookstores and or Google them on their computers and are very likely to soon be into the out and out CCM music, which was the plan from the beginning.

What these unsuspecting people need to know is more about the composers with whom they are being brought into contact. For instance, Townend is a Roman Catholic, and rock and roller in every sense of the word, and is committed to the ecumenical goals. When Townend was asked what kind of music he thought Jesus would listen to if He were on earth today, his answer was "I think he would be doing thrash metal or hip hop or something where we'd go, 'He can't do that!' Because I think he would be challenging our comfortable perceptions. I don't know what He would sing or whose songs He would sing, but I believe He would do it in a way that would surprise and probably shock us." ("What Would Jesus Sing?" from an interview with Stuart Townend, TV series) [34]

It is evident he doesn't know the Jesus of the New Testament. Victor Sears, in *The Baptist Bible Tribune*, in 1981 issued a warning about this kind of music, calling it the "the new Trojan Horse move ... to deaden our churches to spiritual truth."[35] Reader beware!

Reviewing, we are saying CCM music is wrong and should be rejected, not only because of the nature of the music, but also because of ungodly lifestyle of many of the musicians, their ecumenical agenda, and

(3) The Unbiblical doctrine believed and tolerated in CCM: Many examples of this could be cited. Here are three prominent names from CCM: Chris Tomlin, John Michael Talbot, and Stuart Townend.

Roman Catholicism is a major part of CCM. There are many Roman Catholics in the limelight in CCM and many of those who are not RC, work together with others who are. They write songs and perform together. Several of them support the Worship Central training school sponsored by Alpha International, the radically ecumenical charismatic organization that was birthed from the "laughing revival."

The road back to Rome is well-travelled today and the call to return is loud and clear from the RC's and many others. Rick Warren, pastor of the eighth largest church in America and author of the popular *Purpose Driven Church* and similar books that have sold millions of copies, while claiming to be a Baptist, recently sat with a RC priest and broadcast a call for us all to return to Rome in the name of Christian unity. Joel Osteen recently visited with the Pope and praised him for expanding Christianity. Believers need to know what Rome's doctrine is and how CCM music is playing a major role in reuniting all denominations with this heretical religion.

John Michael Talbot, another popular RC, is very dedicated to Mary, says he prays to her faithfully and claims to feel her becoming important in his life.

Regarding the "bridge songs," for a while, the consensus was that CCM was simply wrong and unacceptable. But that has drastically changed. Today the feeling is that such songs can be used in moderation and be safe. The tragic results reveal otherwise. Regarding the leaders in this soft approach, some consider Keith and Kristyn Getty (They team Townend) to be the most dangerous. Some have labeled them "The Pied Pipers of Contemporary Worship Music." Their songs are closer to the traditional hymns. However, as Frank Sells (deceased), my favorite college professor said, "the closer you are to the truth, without having the truth, the greater threat you are to the truth."

Pastors and church leaders, where are you? Paul warned (1 Corinthians 3:11-15), we will answer to God for what kind of material we build on the one foundation of the church, Jesus Christ. If it is gold, silver, and precious stones, it will survive the judgment of fire and we will receive a reward. If it is wood, hay, and stubble, it will go up in smoke. All our labor will be lost and we will suffer loss! What a tragedy for a minister to build a church—even a mega church—only to have it go up in smoke! Jesus warned *many will say to me in that day, Lord, Lord, have we not prophesied in thy name? and in thy name have cast out devils? and in thy name done many wonderful works?"* (Matthew 7:22-23)

What About Using Songs Written by Questionable Authors?

That needs to be considered. We have noted some of the songs written by CCM artists whose lives and doctrine violate scripture and, although the lyrics are true to the Bible and the melody is pleasing, the question remains, should they be used?

If all you consider is the nice music and scriptural words, you will be likely to use such songs as "How Deep the Father's Love for Us." Good men, who have stood for the right music in the past, are now saying there is nothing wrong with using such music. Some quote Charles Spurgeon to shore up their position. It is true that in the introduction to the 1866 *Metropolitan Tabernacle Hymnbook*, Spurgeon said:

> "The area of our researches has been as wide as the bounds of existing religious literature, American and British, Protestant and Romish--ancient and modern. Whatever may be thought of our taste, we have used it without prejudice; and a good hymn has not been rejected because of the character of its author or the heresies of the church in whose hymnal it first occurred. So long as the language and the spirit commended the hymn to our heart, we included it and believe that we have enriched our collection thereby."[36]

Those who know me are aware Spurgeon has been my hero. However, I have differed with him on a number of issues and I differ with him on this one. Instead, I agree with David Cloud's response to those who use Spurgeon's stance to justify using the so-called soft-rock "bridge" songs written by CCM musicians whose life and doctrine are contrary to the Bible. Here is how Cloud addressed this issue:

> "To see the difference between using old Protestant hymns as opposed to borrowing from the world of contemporary worship, all we need to do is consider the fruit. It is drastically different. Not all the great hymn writers of the past were Baptist. There was Fanny Crosby ('He

Hideth My Soul,' Methodist) or James Gray ('Only a Sinner Saved by Grace,' Evangelical Reformed Episcopal) or Martin Luther ('A Mighty Fortress Is Our God,' Lutheran). But they were not heretics out to prey on our children and build a one-world church. They were 'Protestants'— not aligned at all with Roman Catholics nor out to tear down all the doctrinal walls as the stated goal of the CCM crowd today, including those who have written some of the songs mentioned above. Their music has a different beat and motive and is drastically changing the younger generation. The soft music mentioned above is only an introduction to the bigger beat. As we have said, the music, the motive, and the musicians are wrong. Review what we have noted about these musicians. Are these the 'heroes' we need to be putting in front of our young people?"[37]

Pastor, introducing CCM music into your church—even the "bridge songs"—will whet their appetites for more of the music from these musicians and they will be prone to go to the churches where they can get it and the real rock and roll beat. I have seen this happen repeatedly. Most of those who go are young people.   I don't know of one case where that person has become a better Christian because of the change. I have watched them return to their conservative church only to solicit others to join the crowd at the CCM church.

Why Have So Many Embraced This Music?

There are a number of reasons, none of them flattering to God's people. The problem, I believe, lies at the feet of the pastors. Much of the ministry today is woefully ignorant of God's Word. Many are frustrated and defeated. A friend of mine told me some time ago that every preacher he knew was just waiting for the day he could punch out and begin drawing his Social Security.

Discouraged, no heart for lost souls, too scared or too lazy to go after the lost sheep, he is open to anything that might draw people in to pay his salary. It is easy to see how others are doing it. Not because they studied the New Testament (especially the book of Acts) on how the Church reached their generation in about 30 years. Instead, they see how this carnal music is getting a crowd, so they make the change. Sowing to the flesh will always reap corruption. Jesus promised He would build His church. (Matthew 16:18). He will, but not by using fleshly methods. Trust me, you won't like the consequences.

Face It!

Christian Rock would never have existed apart from Rock and Roll.

It is splitting Churches and destroying the doctrine of separation from the world.

It has not produced preachers and missionaries willing to sacrifice for our Savior.

Ask Abraham if he enjoyed resorting to the flesh in an effort to have that promised son instead of waiting on God to do what He had promised. The world is still reeling from that carnal decision!

A Plea to Pastors: If you are determined to try to build a big church in today's world, you are likely to be convinced you will have to go contemporary to do it. It is difficult to find one that is not. However, before you head down that road, let this senior citizen remind you of the words of the great church planter, the Apostle Paul regarding what kind of church you build.

For other foundation can no man lay than that is laid, which is Jesus Christ. (1 Corinthians 3:11-13).

After reminding us we must build on Jesus Christ, the only true foundation, he cautioned us about the kind of material we use to build that church.

There are two distinctly different types of materials—one that is valuable, the gold, silver, and precious stones, and one that is cheap and worthless--the wood, hay, and stubble.

You can build a big pile quickly with wood, hay, and stubble. But after it is tested by divine fire, you will have only ashes! Our goal should not be to build a big church but to be obedient to Christ, the Head of the Church.

Chapter Twelve

Hollywood Movies--Regular and Religious

Concerning how far from the Scriptures these movies usually are, consider a critique by *The Berean Call* regarding the recent *The Son of God* Movie: The following is excerpted from T.A. McMahon, "The Bible According to Hollywood." (April 1, 2014*)*

> "Jesus, the only begotten Son of God, who is the image of the invisible God and the One in whom dwells all the fullness of the Godhead, is not someone who should be portrayed (counterfeited would be more accurate) by a fallen, finite being-- Christian or otherwise. Any such attempt will result in another Jesus, a false Christ. ... Since a host of very influential evangelical leaders ... have been singing the praises of *The Son of God* and the History Channel's Bible series that spawned it, it raises a very serious question regarding *their view of the Bible*. ... Evidently these leaders had no problem with the distortion of the Word in scene after scene. Did the wise men show up at the stable right after the birth of Jesus? Did Jesus entice Peter to follow him by filling his nets with fish? Did Jesus draw the fish into Peter's net by swishing the water with his fingers? Was Mary Magdalene the lone woman among the small band of disciples (if not one of the apostles)? Did Nicodemus play the good Pharisee/bad Pharisee, even challenging Jesus about paying taxes? Was Pilate a brutal military leader who threatened to shut down the temple? Did Jesus have confrontational exchanges with Barabbas? Did Jesus tickle a little girl

and playfully tell her that the temple would be utterly destroyed? At the Last Supper, did Jesus drink the wine that he had just called his own blood? Did the mother of Jesus wash his bloody body in preparation for his burial? Did Jesus *un-symbolically* appear to John on Patmos?

"The list of unbiblical and extra-biblical scenes goes on and on. ... One of the amazing characteristics of visual media is the power of imagery. Scenes that appear on the screen can remain with a viewer, popping into the mind occasionally over his or her lifetime. That can be spiritually devastating. I've heard that some believers who watched Mel Gibson's 'biblical' movie, *The Passion of the Christ*, had great trouble dismissing the face of James Caviezel when their thoughts turned to Jesus, even while in prayer. ... as Dave Hunt and I left the theater after reviewing Mel's movie, I remember Dave {Hunt] crying out to the Lord to remove the imagery of the counterfeit Christ that had just invaded his mind! The Bible doesn't describe Jesus for us in any detail. ... The incredible power of the medium of film resides in its capacity to impact emotions through imagery, acting, dialogue, and music. Tears can flow even in animated movies."[38]

People can have artificial 'life-changing' experiences based upon what they see on the screen, but the Word of God declares: 'the flesh profiteth nothing' (John 6:63). ... Tragically, we are seeing in all of this the words of Peter fulfilled: And through covetousness shall they with feigned words make merchandise of you." (2 Peter 2:3)

Hollywood's religious movies had become popular by the 1960's. About that time I read an article entitled "The Menace of the Religious Movie" by A.W. Tozer (1897-1963), a member of the Christian and Missionary Alliance, a highly respected man of God, with a reputation for personal holiness. The article was needed then and a lot more today.

Tozer noted that while there is nothing wrong with a motion picture, in the wrong hands, it has caused great injury to the Lord's Church. He wrote,

> "No one who values his reputation as a responsible adult will deny that the sex movie and the crime movie have done untold injury to the lives of countless young people in our generation. I am convinced that the modern religious movie is an example of the harmful misuse of a neutral instrument."[39]

We expect that from the world.

But we are addressing the religious movies in which actors attempt to imitate actual, biblical events and make real spiritual truths in front of cameras. Most of these actors are not born again believers and beyond that, God has chosen to deliver us His truth by words, not pictures because that is best. Who dares to think we can improve on God's method? If pictures could have worked better, God could have given us Jesus' whole ministry on film. When God gave the Ten Commandments, we read, *And God spake all these words (Exodus 20:1)* This is the way God has chosen to communicate His truth to us and the way we come to the knowledge of salvation. Notice, it is *He that **heareth** my word, and believeth on him that sent me, hath everlasting life,* (John 5:24 and we are saved by *Faith* [that] *cometh by hearing, and* ***hearing*** *by the word of God.* (Romans 10:17)

There is no way you can accurately convey spiritual truth with pictures. A picture may remind you of some spiritual truth, but it did not convey that truth to you. More often than not, the picture may distract you from the spiritual truth or distort it. Physical truth may be conveyed by picture better by the eye than the ear, but not spiritual truth. Listen to Paul's inspired words: *We look "not at the things which are seen, but at the things which are not seen: for the things which are seen are temporal; but the things which are not seen are eternal.*

(2 Corinthians 4:18).

Consider the fact these religious movies are produced to make money and to entertain. Neither of those are honorable motives for giving out the gospel. They are a type of amusement. Muse means to think. Amuse means not to think.

Giving out God's truth is serious business. Whatever else is required of the speaker, we know he must be genuinely sincere. The subject of acting it out—trying to portray something that is not real to the actor, makes him a hypocrite. It's no accident that the word "hypocrite" comes from the stage. It means **actor,** someone who assumes a character other than his own and plays it for effect. The better he can do it, the better he is as an actor.

Think of any person "acting" like he is praying. Or worse, trying to play the part of Jesus. What he will present would be "another Jesus," rather than the biblical Jesus. The Hollywood film industry has a horrible reputation. You would be hard-pressed to find any segment of society that has a higher percentage of degenerate people in it or has corrupted our country more.

A study of the origin of drama and the theater reveals its roots go back to Greece and worship of the mythical gods. As with all the damaging substitutes that have been invented to try to build God's church, the religious movie can find no warrant for it in scripture. Close scrutiny will reveal the ill effects it has had on the audiences and the actors. We do not dispute the fact it has drawn crowds. We do say the popularity the religious movies have gained could have happened only because the church of

Jesus Christ has lost its fire and become like the Laodicean church in Revelation 3:14-22. Discerning servants of God will tell you as its sales have soared, it has more and more erased the lines of separation scripture sets for God's people to be separate from the world. Many, who have never been to a Hollywood movie, or haven't gone in years, have been lured back into this sin den by first attending religious movies.

Posing the question, "How could this have happened in churches during the last two generations?, Tozer responded "the lazy preacher." He said "The religious movie was the lazy preacher's friend. He could loaf all week and be bailed out when he got the projector running."

Again, Jesus said He would build His church. He will do it through His Holy Spirit infusing holy believers with His power. That will happen when God's people return to the great recipe for revival given in 2 Chronicles 7:14. There are four prerequisites given there—humbling ourselves, prayer, seeking God's face and number four must not be ignored—turning from our wicked ways. Then—and only then will we see genuine revival and God's church built.

In the meantime, man-made carnal substitutes will be promoted. O for a revival that would produce some servants of God with the discernment, and courage to *Cry aloud, spare not, lift up* [their] *voice like a trumpet, and shew my people their transgression, and the house of Jacob their sins.* (Isaiah 58:1)

Chapter Thirteen

Beverage Alcohol

The Lord's Church has confronted many conflicts in the last century. The battle of the Bible. Is it indeed the inspired Word of God? Evolution: Can it be harmonized with the Genesis account of creation? Cooperative evangelism, etc. But the damage done to the church by none of these, in my opinion, compares to that done by the church abandoning its standards of holiness. Concern over this is what has motivated this work. Before I leave this world, I want to do what I can to influence all I can to obey the inspired words of Peter to, *As obedient children, not [to be] fashioning yourselves according to the former lusts in your ignorance, But as he which hath called you is holy, so be ye holy in all manner of conversation, Because as it is written, Be ye holy; for I am holy.* (1 Peter 1:14-16)

Nowhere is this surrender of standards more shocking today than in the area of alcohol. Abandoning its opposition to beverage alcohol is currently the latest evidence of how standards of holiness are dropping. A heartbreaking example is the following:

> "This summer, Moody Bible Institute dropped its 127-year ban against alcohol and tobacco use by faculty and staff. The new emphasis is toward the creation of a 'high trust environment that emphasizes values, not rules.' Spokeswoman Christine Gorz says that

employees must still adhere to all 'biblical absolutes,' but on issues where 'the Bible is not clear, Moody leaves it to employees 'conscience.'"[40]

Many other religious colleges and ministries have done the same in recent years. I am aware of two in our area. One insists that such beverages are not to be consumed from their original containers. In other words, you must pour it into a different container lest some prospective wealthy donor see it and withhold their funds. The other says it must not be consumed in public. What hypocrisy!

Many of those trying to justify the lowering of standards speak of the matters in question as a "gray areas." Such was the case with MBI above. Since they are not forbidden by name in scripture they say they are left to their own conscience to decide whether it is right or not. That argument does not hold water. In Galatians 5:21, after listing a lengthy catalog of sins, Paul added "and such like," meaning anything similar to these. Rather than list everything that was sin or new things that would arise in the future, God gave principles to enable us to make correct judgments. Crack cocaine is not mentioned by name in scripture. Does that mean using it is not a sin?

The Bible teaches believers' their bodies are *the temple of the Holy Ghost which is in you, which ye have of God, and ye are not your own, For ye are bought with a price: therefore glorify God in your body, and in your spirit, which are God's.* (1 Corinthians 6:19-20) The same passage also reminds us our *bodies are members of Christ.* (Verse 15). We are left on earth in these bodies to serve and glorify Christ and we cannot serve Him without them. What if we abuse our bodies and die young? We have destroyed God's property and robbed Him of His rightful glory. That is sin. The principle is clear: Whatever harms the body is sin whether it is named in scripture or not.

But some would say, "O, but drinking alcohol in moderation does not harm the body, but even helps it." The liquor industry would like for you to believe that, but consider this: "Alcohol 'Benefits' Are A Myth: A new study by medical researchers in Oregon disputes a recent Harvard report of health benefits from alcohol-- that moderate drinking reduces heart attacks. The Oregon study says that alcohol in fact depresses heart function, and says: 'Alcohol is a toxic substance--a poison--and shouldn't be used for health.'(1/3 Huntsville Times). Misuse of alcohol accounts for 100,000 deaths each year, and about 18 million Americans suffer from alcohol dependency. About 76 million people are affected by alcohol abuse at some time. In 1992, at least 347 of Alabama's 1,031 traffic fatalities, or thirty-four percent, were attributed to drunk drivers. Alcohol is a killer!'"[41]

If you still choose to insist drinking in moderation is okay, just so you don't drink too much and get addicted, let me tell you, if you never take the first drink, you will never get addicted. A country preacher years ago said, "A dram drinker is as much akin to a drunk as a pig is a hog. Just give him time and he'll prove it." People don't plan to become drunks. They think they can handle it.

Our culture is drowning in this "devil in liquid form." Throw out the so-called "legalism" of saying drinking beverage alcohol is sin and you will add to the misery and devastation this sin is causing. Yes, and as with all sin, you will answer to God for it.

The curse of this sin is serious business today and believer, you need to know the pressure is growing for us to capitulate.

While in the past, the tendency to sanction drinking alcohol was mainly from more liturgical denominations, that is not the case today. David Cloud notes it is coming from men who profess to be Evangelicals.

> "For example, the book *Listening to the Beliefs of Emerging Churches: Five Perspectives* contains probably a dozen references to the joys of drinking. The contributors are Karen Ward, Mark Driscoll, John Burke, Dan Kimball, and Doug Pagitt. They meet in bars and taverns for theological discussions, and they exchange beer-making techniques."[42]

Here are some things we all need to know regarding this issue.

The word *wine* in the Bible may mean anything from the juice that is still in the grape to something that will make you drunk. It is sometimes called the "fruit of the vine."

The many warnings in scripture against all the misery and consequences of drinking alcohol should make us very reluctant to ever take the first drink. (See Proverbs 23:29-35)

Scripture instructs us to not even be among wine bibbers and not to "look on it" when it sparkling and fizzling--when it is intoxicating.

Since Jesus never violated any truth in the Bible, those claiming He made fermented wine in John 2 have a problem when they teach that's what He made, especially since He made so much of it (about 180 gallons), making it possible for many to get drunk. No one should say they have a right to make and drink wine because Jesus did unless they can prove the wine they are drinking is the same as what He made.

What Jesus gave His apostles to drink at the Last supper that represented His blood that was about to be shed <u>is never called wine</u>, but instead, it is always called the "fruit of the vine."

> The late Dr. Bruce Lackey said, "The context will always show when 'wine' refers to alcoholic beverages. In such cases, God discusses the bad effects of it and warns against it. An example would be Genesis 9, which describes Noah's experience after the Flood. Verse 21 states 'and he drank of the wine, and was drunken,' clearly refers to alcoholic beverage."[43]

In 2014, the World Health Organization reported that 3.3 million people die each year because of alcohol. That's more than die of AIDS, tuberculosis, and violence combined, including drunk driving, alcohol induced violence and abuse, and a multitude of diseases and disorders. Alcohol causes one is 20 deaths globally every year.

Since many who have been enslaved to alcohol, have relapsed and gone back to it by being enticed to take one drink, no church should serve fermented wine at the communion service. Roman Catholics do and they have homes for priests who are hooked on booze.

Alcohol and Adultery are twin sins. God links them and pronounces a curse on both: *Woe unto him that giveth his neighbour drink that puttest thy bottle to him, and makest him drunken also, that thou mayest look on their nakedness.*

(Habakkuk 2:15) This is a warning against all those who serve it and to those who may be victims of the lustful opposite sex who serves them liquor to gain their lustful ways.

In these six decades in the ministry, in the hospitals, jails, prisons, the courts, at funerals, and especially in the homes, I have seen up close what this sin can do. I have heard all the arguments in favor of making and marketing this curse on God's creation, and how the drunks (not alcoholics as they prefer) say they are "sick" and can't help it. But after trying to help feed families because their funds have been spent on booze, helping find places for kids because of the same problem, hauling them down to the Union Mission, coming between a drunken, violent father and his children to protect them, wrestling with one to get him in my car to take him home, only to have his mother refuse to let me bring him in, and have one tell me he was going to kill me, I still go when I'm called because they need the Lord and not the liquor.

God has protected me and given some victories. A recent case is a man whom I visited for thirty years. He once sent me word he would kill me if I came back again. I continued to go, but never once got him in church to preach to him. However, it was my privilege to see him give his heart to Jesus just thirty-two days before he died. During those last few days, he gave good evidence he was a changed man.

As is the case with many drunks, he had been abusive to his wife. Two days after he received Christ as Savior, he told her that she was the most wonderful wife in the whole world. She called me and said, "Preacher, I have never heard anything close to that from that man in forty years!" Instead of sadness, there was joy in that family and in my heart and others when I stood behind his casket and preached his funeral. I expect to meet him in heaven. Thank you Jesus!

As a postscript, Leviticus 10 furnishes a vivid reminder of how serious God is regarding liquor. Learn here it has no place in His service or in His servants. Two sons of Aaron, the High Priest, were burned with fire from God when they presumed to take matters into their own hands and offer strange (profane) fire before the Lord. The two verses following state that *The Lord spake unto Aaron, saying, Do not drink wine nor strong drink, thou, nor thy sons with thee, when ye go into the tabernacle of the congregation, lest ye die: it shall be a statute forever throughout your generations.* (Leviticus 10:8-9) Commentators believe that this prohibition, coming at this time, suggests that Nadab and Abihu were drunk.

A Funny: My good friend, Dr. Royce Thomason (deceased), who published the *Voice in the Wilderness* for many years, once told me my writings were rather "heavy" and advised me to drop in a little humor now and then. Here is one I received from Dr. R. G. Lee (deceased), longtime pastor of Bellevue Baptist Church in Memphis, TN. Two of us were visiting with him in his humble home in about 1973 when he shared the following with us regarding drinking liquor.

"Jack and Jill went up the hill to get some moonshine liquor, Jack went blind and lost his mind and Jill was even sicker."

Chapter 14

GAMBLING

The predatory business of gambling is mushrooming. Eighty-five percent of U.S. adults have gambled at least once in their lives, eighty percent in the past year. (National Problem Gambling Awareness Week, January 2011.) More than we want to admit, some in our churches may be included in that statistic.

Not so long ago, a Texas pastor and a member of his church where I was scheduled to preach, picked me up at the airport. Riding alone in the backseat, I was surprised to see the stub from a lottery ticket. There have been stories on TV of even pastors who have preached that gambling is wrong, but when they won big bucks playing the lottery, they backtracked and said God was just supplying their needs.

State sponsored lotteries and the great number of legalized Casinos are at the heart of this business. The recent fiscal downturn led cash-strapped state lawmakers to seek unconventional revenue-raising alternatives. Many turned to state sponsored gambling. Now they are learning rarely are they as lucrative, or as long-lasting, as supporters claim. Still, some kind of government sanctioned gambling is now allowed in all but two states. Forty-three states plus the District of Columbia have state lotteries.

The public is often told proceeds from gambling will help pay for things like schools. Close examination, we are told, too often reveals, funds that were promised to schools are transferred to other purposes. Consider also what gambling is teaching our children: "You don't have to work. You can gamble and strike it rich!"

We all know, there are few who hit the jackpot, and studies of those who do are alarming. If their winnings are sizeable, they often quit their jobs, quickly squander the money, and then, out of work and unable to find a job, robbery or suicide may follow. Also, gambling invariably leads to more cost for things like welfare, police protection, and jails, not to speak of what the loss of income does to families, decreasing their quality of life.

What Is Gambling?

Gambling is legal in most of the USA today, but not legal with a holy God. So what is there about gambling that makes it wrong? Endeavoring to excuse the sin of gambling, you may hear people say, "Well, it's just a game of chance. Everything's a gamble. Farming is a gamble. You never know if you're going to win or lose."

Yes, you can lose at farming. But there are two big differences: (1) When you win at gambling, someone has to lose. Not so with farming. Usually, if one farmer has a good crop, others do also. The same when he loses. (2) With farming, you work expecting to make a profit. That is not true with gambling. You don't work. You hope to gain without working. You produce no goods or services but hope to get money. That is wrong. That is the sin of covetousness. God's Word teaches, *Let him that stole steal no more: but rather let him labour, working with his hands the thing which is good, that he may have to give to him that needeth.* (Ephesians 4:28) Since Adam and Eve were ejected from Eden, God has ordained that men are to work. Paul reminded the believers at Thessalonica *for even when we were with you, this we commanded you, that if any would not work, neither should he eat.* (2 Thessalonians 3:10) Not if they "could not work" but if they would not work.

Clearly evident to any rational person is the fact that gambling is wrong. It is a parasite on society. Collectively, socially, and in all kinds of ways, everybody loses. If there is such a thing as the sin of covetousness, this is it. When America had higher morals and more character, gambling was illegal in most places. As morals have nosedived, this evil has increased. Christian, let this sin never be named among us. That includes raffles also. When you pay money hoping to win more, that is gambling, That is true of things like buying raffle tickets and fishing tournaments where you pay a fee hoping to win the jackpot. We ought to hate this sin. Charles Spurgeon once said, regarding the soldiers gambling for Jesus' garments at the foot of His Cross, "How could any Christian ever pick up a pair of dice after seeing that scene?"

A comment by the former Secretary of Education, Bill Bennett (2003) regarding his problem with gambling was "Gambling's not a sin in my Church." Mr. Bennett and all of us need to know, it doesn't matter what your church says about this sin or any other sin. They don't make the rules. Our Creator makes them and He has recorded them for us for our good. No, there is not a verse that says gambling is a sin, but there are plenty that teach covetousness is and covetousness is the root of gambling. Also, like other sins, studies show gamblers are more likely to smoke, drink, and do drugs. And, like other sins, it is addictive. There is an epidemic of gambling addicts in our nation today. You can bet on it. Gambling is a Bad Bet! We all need to shun it and that includes the older generation who are increasingly succumbing to this enticing evil.

Chapter Fifteen

Loving Jesus – The Key to Holy Living

Simon, son of Jonas, lovest thou me? (John 21:16)

O thou whom my soul loveth. (Song of Solomon 1:7)

There are other issues that Christians will confront that could be addressed. With the help of the Holy Spirit, which all believers have (Romans 8:9), a good understanding of scripture, and a heart truly desirous to do (not just know) the will of God, every Christian has God's promise that He will reveal His will to them.

Consider Proverbs 3:5-6: *Trust in the Lord with all thine heart; and lean not unto thine own understanding. In all thy ways acknowledge him, and he shall direct thy paths.*

The promise here is that **dedication gives discernment**. For those issues not specifically named in scripture, God will reveal His will to the heart willing to do His will. John 7:17 says He will do that regarding doctrine. It follows He will also do it on these moral issues. Philippians 3:15 makes the same promise to the yielded heart. New Testament believers are treated as adult sons, who should not have to be told what to do by someone like a priest. (Galatians 4:1ff) As we grow we understand these things better. However, maturity does not mean we grow away from those basic, unchanging moral principles that never change.

Let us come now to the question that must be answered.

"What has to happen in our hearts to truly motivate us to live the kind of holy lives our Lord asks us to live?" We can study and say we agree with all that has been said and still fail. The issue revolves, not around how much we know, but how much we really love Jesus. Holy living grows out of a deep love to our Savior. So what is there about Him that generates that kind of deep love?

Jesus' parable of the two debtors gives some insight. He told of a creditor forgiving one man a small debt and another a huge amount. Neither debtor had the means to repaying their debt. They both made the same plea. Both were freely forgiven. (Luke 7:40-43) Jesus asked His host, Simon, a Pharisee, which debtor would love the creditor the most? Simon, rightly said, it would be the one who was forgiven the larger indebtedness.

What prompted Jesus to give this parable was a woman who was a "sinner"—a prostitute, knowing Jesus was in the house, came in weeping. With an alabaster flask of expensive ointment she began to wash His feet with her tears, wipe them with her hair, and anoint them with the ointment. Simon, who had invited Jesus to his home to try to learn if Jesus truly was a prophet, decided Jesus was a fake or He would have known what kind of woman this was and would not have let her touch Him.

Jesus then turned to the woman and said to Simon, *Seest thou this woman? I entered into thine house, thou gavest me no water for my feet: but she hath washed my feet with tears, and wiped them with the hairs of her head.*

Simon surely felt the sting. He had not been forgiven much because, typical of a Pharisee, he didn't think he had much for which he needed to be forgiven. So, forgiven little, he loved little. Conversely, the woman of ill-repute, so conscious and ashamed of her sin, she sobbed out her heart to Jesus and experienced His forgiveness.. Forgiven much, she now loved Him much.

If you, dear readers, are resisting obeying Jesus on moral issues, you need to face your own heart and ask yourself, "Is my problem I just don't love Jesus like I should?" Informed, godly believers do not argue about these issues. Their love for Jesus causes them to view these so-called sacrifices as Paul did. All he gave up he considered nothing but "dung" [rubbish]! (Philippians 3:8.) They love Him. John told us why. We love *him, because he first loved us.* (1 John 4:19) They understand the awesome price He paid to reveal His love and redeem them from hell!

Read what Paul suffered in serving Jesus and let the great apostle tell you why he gladly bore it all. He said, it was because he loved Jesus, the *Son of God, who loved **me**, and gave himself for **me**.* (Galatians 2:20) "Me!" Yes, me the murderer of Christians!

In scripture, you don't hear the true servants of God whining about all they had to give up. They were more like a man in Tennessee I heard years ago. He said, "When I got saved, I didn't have to give up a thing. I just got shed of some things."

Consider the verse above where the bride in that great love story says to her spouse, *O thou whom my soul loveth.* (Song of Solomon 1:7) She loved him. Not just his gifts, but him.

> "My Jesus I love **Thee,**
> I know **Thou** art mine,
> For **Thee** all the follies,
> Of sin I resign."
> --William R. Featherson

She was confident she loved him and only him. Imagine your mate telling you she hoped she loved you. Or, as a song from the past said, "Two loves have I. To one I am tied, to the other I am true." Nonsense! Love is an exclusive thing. Christian, Christ must be the only One our souls love. He tolerates no competitor. And remember, if you are going to influence others for Christ, your love for Him must be passionate. We don't pass on to others things we just talk about nonchalantly.

Can you say that your love for Him is that kind of love? Or do you identify more with those in the Ephesian church who had "left their first love." (Revelation 2:4) Does an honest inventory of your heart cause you concern? If so, you are not alone. To many,

> There is a Question comes to me,
> Oft it gives me anxious thought,
> Do I love the Lord or no?
> Am I His or am I not?
> --Charles Spurgeon

Addressing Peter, Jesus pressed the vital question, *Simon, son of Jonas, lovest thou me?* (John 21:16)

Jesus was soon to return to His Father in heaven. He was preparing His followers for the task for which He had saved and trained them. Would they be faithful to do it? The answer to this question would determine that.

He did not ask Peter, "Do you believe I am the Christ? Are you willing to preach the gospel? "Do you promise to quit cursing?" All those issues would be settled if he could honestly say he loved Jesus. He had told Jesus he was willing to die for Him. His brag was bogus. The matter of heart-love had to be settled **now!** In Jesus presence. In front of his peers. In his own heart.

Jesus told him there were tough times ahead. (John 21:18) Only genuine heart-love would enable him to stay true to his Lord. This very personal question from Jesus needs to be answered by each of us now because, the best Bible students I know believe tough times are ahead for us.

Considering what it means to truly love God, we need to understand love is not some abstract, emotional feeling. If it is real it acts. It gives. *God so loved the world that he **gave** his only begotten Son.* (John 3:16) Love gives and love obeys. Jesus said if we love Him we will obey Him. (John 14:15, 23) Only to those who obey Him does He give the Holy Spirit who is essential if we are to be effective in His service. (Acts 5:32)

Does your love for Jesus show? Do you seek Him in His Word and in prayer? Prayer and the Bible are what make His presence real to us. Routinely reading a chapter and praying cold prayers do not characterize those who can say *O thou whom my soul loveth,* (Song of Solomon 1:7) because,

"You may as well kneel down to gods of wood and stone
As offer to the living God a prayer of words alone."

Many have proven their love by sealing their testimonies with their blood. As I am writing this manuscript, the world is hearing almost daily of Christians who are being brutally martyred—beheaded --rather than deny their Savior. Unbelievers are prone to say, "What a waste!" "Why would anyone be so foolish as to die rather than change religions?" Believers know why. We know what He did for us. Many who have known His love have loved him in return and paid the ultimate price.

Often I have been blessed reading of the death of Christian martyrs like those in England in the 1500's. I agree with J.C Ryle who said, he wanted the names of all these martyrs to be "household words"' in every Protestant family throughout the land. Teaching a course I entitled "Motivated by the Martyrs," I was often, humbled by how little I have done to show Jesus that

I really do love him.

One name I will share here that especially moved me was that of Bishop Thomas Cranmer, burned at the stake in   1557. He lived in tumultuous times when King Henry VIII broke away from the Pope of Rome and set up the Church of England. He appointed Thomas Cranmer as the Archbishop of Canterbury, the spiritual director.

The position did not prove to be as grand as it might have seemed. While Henry VIII reigned, Cranmer was a great help to the growing reformation. Edward VI followed and during his brief reign Cranmer was in the forefront of the reformation. Then, suddenly King Edward VI died and Mary—Yes, "Bloody Mary," Queen of Scots, in conjunction with the king of France whom she had married, ascended the throne. Roman Catholicism was back with a vengeance.

Friends urged Cranmer to flee, but he chose to stay. Soon, like many ministers, he was arrested, charged with heresy and imprisoned. Trial followed trial until, promising him freedom, they succeeded in getting him to sign a limited recantation. They had no intention of honoring that promise.

He soon learned of his impending execution. The Romanist expected him to repeat his "confession." That did not happen. Instead, He calmly spoke to the crowd, and asked them to pray God for the forgiveness of his sins, one of which especially grieved his conscience. Referring to the time he signed that recantation, he said, "And now I come to the great thing which troubles my conscience more than anything I ever said or did in my whole life, and that is, the setting abroad of writings contrary to the truth, which now here I renounce and refuse, as things written for fear of death, and to save my life... And forasmuch as my hand offended in writing contrary to my heart, my hand shall first be punished."[44]

He had time only to denounce the Pope and their claim that the sacrament of the Mass was the literal body of Christ. This so angered the Romanists they immediately pulled him off the stage and hurried him to the stake.

Overcoming his natural weakness, with cheerful countenance, he stepped barefooted to the stake. Then followed this amazing scene:

> "Cranmer, stretching out his right hand, said, 'This is the hand that wrote it, and therefore it shall suffer punishment first.' When the flames rose up, he held out his hand to meet them, retaining it steadfastly, so that the people saw that it was burning before the fire reached any other part of his body; while he repeatedly exclaimed, with a loud and firm voice, 'this hand hath offended! This unworthy right hand!' 'Never,' says Southey, 'did martyr endure the fire with more invincible resolution;' no cry was heard from him, save the exclamation of the proto-martyr Stephen, 'Lord Jesus, receive my spirit!' He stood immovable at the stake to which he was bound, --his countenance raised, looking up to heaven, and anticipating that rest on which he was about to enter; and thus, in the greatness of the flame, he yielded up his spirit. The fire soon did its work, and his heart was found unconsumed amidst the ashes."[45]

We stand in awe of such a manifestation of love for the

Savior! But that pales in comparison to Jesus' love for us. From the closing chapters of the gospels, we are told enough to overwhelm us and give us every reason to love Him forever. The more we read of the agonies He endured on Calvary, the more those images are indelibly seared into our consciousness.

Who can stand on Golgotha and hear Him mocked, see His hands and feet nailed to the tree, His side pierced so deeply we can see all the way to His great heart—who can see that and ever be the same? And what of those three hours of darkness when we could see nothing, but could only hear His heart-rending cries as He took our hell to give us His heaven? Nothing—nothing else in the entire universe moves us as that gruesome sight! More than most the beloved John understood something of this when he wrote, *We love him because he first loved us.* (1 John 4:19)

Spurgeon knew much of His love and could express it like few others. He wrote, "My life, when it shall ebb out, may cause me to lose many mental powers, but memory will love no other name than is recorded there. The agonies of Christ have burnt His name into our hearts; you cannot stand and see Him mocked by Herod's men of war, you cannot behold Him made nothing of, and spit upon by menial lips, you cannot see Him with the nails pierced through His hands and through His feet, you cannot mark Him in the extreme agonies of His awful passion without saying, 'And did You suffer all this for *me?*'

"Then I must love You, Jesus. My heart feels that no other can have such a claim upon it as You have, for none others have spent themselves for me as You have done. Others may have sought to buy my love with the silver of earthly affection, and with the gold of a zealous and affectionate character, but You have bought it with Your precious blood, and You have the richest claim to it— Yours shall it be and that forever!"[46]

Learn of this love and all the complaining about those worldly issues will vanish and we can sincerely sing

When I Survey the Wondrous Cross,
On Which the Prince of glory died,
My Richest gain I count but loss,
And pour contempt on all my pride.
--Isaac Watts

Dear friend, our love is all that our God has asked of us. He summed it up by saying, *Thou shalt love the Lord thy God with all thy heart, and with all thy soul, and with all thy mind. This is the first and great commandment.* (Matthew 22:37-38) We have every reason to love Him and no reason not to. No wonder Paul wrote *If any man love not the Lord Jesus Christ, let him be Anathema Maranatha.* (1 Corinthians 16:22)

Endnotes and Bibliography

1. Published by Andy Neckar, Vol. 8, Number 2. March-April., 2003

2. Spurgeon Charles H. The Metropolitan Tabernacle Pulpit, Volume 50, Sermon, 2902. Pilgrim Publishers, Pasadena, Texas 77501.

3. Fundamental Baptist Information Service, P.O. Box 610368, Port Huron, MI 48061, wayoflife.org)

4. Spurgeon, Charles H. The Metropolitan Tabernacle Pulpit Volume 16 Sermon 965 Pilgrim Publications, Pasadena, Texas 77501

5. Edersheim, Alfred History of the Old Testament, Book 2, chapter 8, studylight.org

6. Spurgeon, Charles Metropolitan Tabernacle Pulpit Proverbs 11:30 Pilgrim Publications, Pasadena, Texas 77501

7. Surgeon, Charles The New Park Street Pulpit No. 89 Pilgrim Publications, Pasadena, Texas 77501

8. D.L. Moody, "The Overcoming Life and Other Sermons, 1896).www.wayoflife12.13.2013

9. DeHaan, M. R. The Tabernacle, 1955). December 13, 2013, www.wayoflife.org, fbns@wayoflife.org

10. Fundamental Baptist Information Service, P.O. Box 610368, Port Huron, MI 48061, wayoflife.org)

11. Edersheim, Alfred History of the Old Testament, Vol. 1, Genesis 3, studylight.org

12. www.christianity.com/

13. Wardlaw, R. Biblical Illustrator, Volume 17, Page 609 Baker Book House, Grand Rapids, MI 49506

14. Biblical Illustrator, Genesis

15. Beecher, Henry Ward Thomas W. Handford - 1887

16. Brooks, Thomas (1608 – 1680 https://crazycalvinistponderizes.wordpress.com

17. Hale, Sir Matthew 1609 Naval Journal, Volumes 17-18 Page 227)

18. *Fundamental Baptist Information Service, P.O. Box 610368, Port Huron, MI 48061,December 30, 2011*

19. *Ibid, 12/25/09*

20. *Ibid, October 8, 1998*

21. *Joel Dreyfuss, Witchita Eagle, 10-6-1970, in Fundamental Baptist Information Service, P.O. Box 610368, Port Huron, MI 48061, , 6/13 06:*

22.. *Ibid, May/21/13 06:03*

23. *Ibid*

24. *Glover, Attorney Voyle Biblical Evangelist 5-7-2014*

25. *CC 6-1-96*

26. *Fundamental Baptist Information Service, P.O. Box 610368, Port Huron, MI 48061, March, 2004*

27. *Garlock, Dr. Frank, used by permission*

28. *Sears, Evangelist Gordon, Songfest newsletter, April 2001*

29. *CC 6-15-1994*

30. *www.keithhunt.com/Rockin.html*

31. *wayoflife.org/friday_church_news/15_18.phpVol 15, Issue 18 - May 2, 2014 and June 3, 2014*

32. *Fundamental Baptist Information Service, P.O. Box 610368, Port Huron, MI 48061, Jul/09/14*

33. *Ibid October 17, 2011*

34. *wayoflife.org Feb/28/13*

35. *Sears, Victor The Baptist Bible Tribune, in 1981*

36. *1866 Metropolitan Tabernacle Hymnbook,*

37. *wayoflife.org Sep/24/13*

38. *The Berean Call, PO Box 7019 Bend OR 97708.*

39. *Tozer, A.W., Worship and Entertainment .it contains the essay "The Menace of the Religious Movie."Published by WingSpread.*

40. *Christianity Today, Sept.20, 2013). www.christianitytoday.com*

41. *CC 1-15-94*

42. *Fundamental Baptist Information Service, P.O. Box 610368, Port Huron, MI 4806 November 12, 2013*

43. *Lackey, Dr. Bruce. wayoflife.org/otimothy_08/2014*

44. *Last Days of the Martyrs* by Andrew R. Bonar, permission kindly granted by John Ritchie Ltd
45. *Ibid*
46. Spurgeon, Charles *New Park Street Pulpit, Volume 6 Number 338* Pilgrim Publications, Pasadena, Texas 77501

Key Sources and Acknowledgements

CC Calvary Contender Jerry Huffman, Huntsville, AL. *(Deceased) The following is a tribute to him written by his pastor and included in the final issue of the Calvary Contender, December 2005. Having read his publication or many years and talked to him a number of times, I can say a hearty "Amen" to the tribute below.*

For twenty-three years Jerry Huffman has been "warning and informing" through the Calvary Contender. The CC has been a beacon of light for many of us in the ministry. There is no way of estimating how many preachers as well as laymen that Brother Huffman, through the CC, has influenced to stand strong against compromise and the subtle drift we see in Christendom.

It takes a certain type of man to read over 100 periodicals each month and pick and condense the real issues into a two-page paper. I have been Jerry's pastor since 1979. For those of us who know him personally, we would all agree that Jerry has the most tender and sweet spirit of any believer anywhere. He has no ax to grind with anyone. He is a man who, when he sees compromise, does not get mad and become hateful but grieves because the cause of Christ is hurt. He has been and is a gentleman, a giant of a Christian, who has served all of us faithfully over the years. His only desire is to see God's people standing without compromise, serving the Lord and being faithful to the Word of God. (Dr. Greg McLaughlin)

O Timothy and wayoflife.org David Cloud (1949) He is the man behind these publications. Born into a Christian family, but lived in sin until age 23. After conversion he attended Tennessee Temple Bible School. He has spent 20 years in South Asia as a church planting missionary. Within six months after his conversion he had printed his first book, warning about rock and roll music. He has spent an average of at least six hours per day in study since his conversion. He has built a 6,000-volume research library, especially strong in the areas of church history, the history of the Bible, ecumenism, theological modernism, New Evangelicalism, Fundamentalism, the Pentecostal-Charismatic movement, contemporary Christian music, and the Roman Catholic Church.

His web-site offers many books, videos, and free eBooks on timely subjects from a well-informed conservative believer. I am greatly indebted to him for information for this book.

Abbreviations used in this material;

- *Christian News CN: 684 Luther Dr. New Haven, MO 63068*
- *Calvary Contender CC http://home.hiwaay.net/~contendr/ no longer being published*
- *David Cloud, Fundamental Baptist Information Service, P.O. Box 610368, Port Huron, MI 48061, wayoflife.org*

- *biblicalevangelist.org Editor Robert Sumner, 5717 Pine Drive, Raleigh, NC 27606The Berean Call, PO Box 7019 Bend OR 97708*

Holiness Demanded

Made in the USA
Lexington, KY
23 December 2014